Hand-Shaped Art

by
Diane Bonica

illustrated by Jan Renard

Cover by Kathryn Hyndman

GOOD APPLE, INC.
BOX 299
CARTHAGE, IL 62321-0299

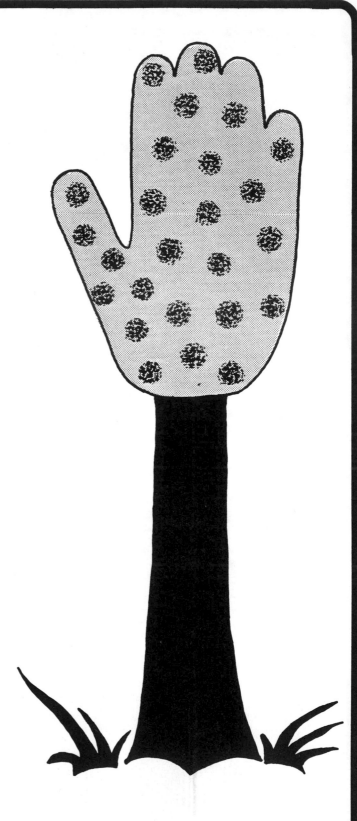

Dedication

To all the little hands that inspired me, especially those belonging to Ashley, Adam and Andrew

and to Mrs. Ann Carey who taught me my first handprint.

GA1079

This art book is the result of something that I learned in kindergarten . . . a simple hand turkey. I remember how proficient I felt being able to make that turkey over and over again, away from school and without help. My five-year-old art skills have failed me in many situations but never with that handy fellow. I always had with me all the tools that I needed to make him perfectly. He was my success builder . . . my drawing partner.

When I became a kindergarten teacher, I decided to find some equally successful art projects for my students. I wanted them to have a drawing partner that would allow them to feel like a successful artist. I wondered, "If a hand could become a Thanksgiving turkey, what other possibilities might exist?" Never did I expect to find that the hand could be the basic form for so many projects. The human hand is so versatile. It can be turned, twisted, trimmed, stretched and folded to create anything from a January snowflake to a June sailboat. My kindergarten classroom became filled with happy hand artists. The children delighted in transforming a part of themselves into a successful seasonal craft project. You see, they became part of the art.

Parents were delighted to receive any and all crafts that incorporated a handprint of their favorite artist. Hand butterflies, bunnies, boats, ballerinas, blossoms and birds became treasured masterpieces destined for family scrapbooks.

Now, as a mother of three preschoolers, I join the ranks of the "ooers" and "aaah'ers" as these projects preserve the hands of my little ones. I must confess, however, that children are somewhat hesitant about getting their hands too close to me for fear I'll start inventing some additional artful transformations.

Diane Bonica

GA1079

Table of Contents

Handy Hints About Handprints

There are three methods of hand painting outlined in this book. The first is a simple trace and cutout system. The second method involves tracing and coloring. The third avenue requires that paint be applied directly onto the hands of students. Almost every handprint can be done using each of these three methods. I have outlined my favorite method for each project. You may wish to try another one. No matter how you manage each handprinting session, expect a lot of smiles from your students. The children love these activities and they will want to do MORE! Remind budding artists that handprint art should always end up on paper. For some odd reason, moms and school janitors don't appreciate this unique art on walls or classroom doors.

The trace and cutout system is very neat and easy to master. Cleanup is minimal and students in grades one through three can usually work independently or in pairs. The handprint is simply traced onto paper that is already the color of the object that you wish to create, for example, brown paper for a nest or a Columbus ship or green paper for a frog or a spring leaf. If your handprint art is to be an independent activity, your students will need to practice hand placement to insure a recognizable print. Some hand configurations are a bit awkward at first but *they all do work*! Using a rubber band to join fingers is a great help. Children in kindergarten and younger classes will require assistance with tracing and cutting out their prints. Upper level students or parent helpers can supply the support needed for these young artists. Once the handprint has been cut out, it is usually glued onto background paper and details are added with crayons or markers. Your finished print is then ready for display.

The trace and color method is employed when the item created is not a solid color. The dress for the autumn dancer (page 64) is traced on drawing paper and the fall colors are added with crayons or markers. Cleanup for this procedure is simple and quick to accomplish. Young students like this method because they can readily re-create it on their own (for example, the famous hand turkey).

As you might expect, hand painting is a messy activity. Picturing twenty-five four-year-olds with red painted hands is enough to make any teacher faint! Here are some helpful hints to minimize the "messiness" and allow the fun and learning to happen.

To control paint drippings, it is best to have each hand painting activity under adult supervision. Your work area should be protected with an old tablecloth or a covering of newspaper. The adult can sit or stand while applying the paint to the child's hand. It is best for the student to remain standing to allow for firm pressure on each print. The activity is a fluid one. First, the adult applies the paint onto the student's palm, using a paintbrush. The student then makes the print by pressing his palm onto the paper; hands are then thoroughly washed and dried while the print is drying. Lastly additional items are drawn in to create the finished product. The prints are practically dry once they are made, but the additional drying time during cleanup is helpful before adding legs to bugs and spots to butterflies, etc. One adult can work with two children at a time. The second child's print is made while the first child is washing up. Working in this fashion, a class of 24-28 students can be finished in about an hour.

It is truly fun for both the adult and child to share these creative ventures. Painting directly onto a child's palm is often a ticklish, laughable experience. It is a golden opportunity to experiment with art and language. Little artists are full of words when they are lending their hands as canvases. With children under six the adult may also wish to aid in the printmaking itself by applying additional pressure to the child's hand as it is placed onto the paper. Sometimes little fingers are too light to make a bold print. The extra touch of a "big person" can help.

GA1079

Tempera paint, made according to directions on the jar, is the perfect medium for hand painting. The tempera colors give vibrant prints. Immediate handwashing is required with this paint. Students should wear aprons and sleeves must be rolled high. Hand soap and warm water work great. If you don't have an in-house sink in your classroom, a dishpan of warm soapy water will be fine. Remember to have lots of paper towels for drying too. Prints made with tempera paint work best on drawing paper or construction paper. The thickness of these papers absorbs the paint without wrinkling or bleeding through.

Watercolor paints may also be used for hand painting. There needs to be lots of paint on each brush and a minimum of water for good color. The painted hand should be wet but never dripping. Prints made with watercolors can be applied to construction paper and typing paper. The latter is easier on the supply budget.

Hand painting can also be accomplished by dipping hands in paint. Handprints done in this fashion are similar to those in method one—they are mono-colored—except for the "trimmings." To make dip prints, pour tempera paint into a pie tin or cookie sheet (works great when two hands are being painted). The paint should barely cover the bottom of the pans. The child then places his palm in the paint and then onto the paper. Too much paint causes unnecessary dripping. Just enough paint makes for perfect prints. Kindergartners who have done adult-directed handprinting can do hand dipping independently. Make certain that handwashing facilities are close by and readily available.

Handprint art is sure to find a welcomed home in your classroom's curriculum. It is learning that is guaranteed to make you and your students smile. And who knows—maybe the hand you paint today may be the one to sign the world Peace Treaty tomorrow. Happy Painting . . . Happy Printing!

GA1079

Snowfuls

MATERIALS: six sheets of white typing paper (5" x 7"), three white drinking straws, scissors, glue, thin wire or fishing line

PROCEDURE: Trace hand (fingers extended) and cut out six prints for each child.

Fold each hand, fingers too, and cut designs as you would to create a paper snowflake.

Use short length of wire to tie the three straws together in the center. Separate the straws.

Glue a snowflake hand to the end of each straw.

Mount each completed snowflake on a piece of blue or black construction paper or hang about the classroom using fishing line.

OPTION: Tape completed snowflake hands to the windows.

BOOKS TO ENJOY: *The Snowman* by Raymond Briggs, 1986, Random.

Fun in the Snow by Laura Damon, 1987, Troll Assoc.

GA1079

BULLETIN BOARD:

Use a large sheet of blue or black paper to create the background. Sponge paint the background with 2″ circular sponge shapes that have been dipped in a solution of white paint and white glue. Dust the painted areas with granulated sugar to add sparkle.

Attach student-made snowflakes and samples of student writing. Some snowflakes could be hung from the ceiling in front of the bulletin board.

ACTIVITY:

Use Mother Nature's white fluff as your wintry easel. After a snowstorm take your class outside with watercolors and brushes. Sculp snow statues and paint in colorful details. A dabbing motion works best with your brush. Invite other classes to admire your colorful winter masterpieces.

If you live in a more temperate climate and don't have Mother Nature's natural white fluff, you can improvise with shaved ice. Make a snow cone for each student and color with colored syrup. The effect may not be as eye-appealing as the outdoor winter art gallery but the taste will definitely be more delicious.

GA1079

Enough White Stuff

MATERIALS: 9" x 12" piece of black paper, various colors of construction paper scraps, two 5" x 7" pieces of white paper, white paint, glue, water, sugar

PROCEDURE: Use the various colors of construction paper scraps to make a house. Glue these pieces to the sheet of black construction paper.

Trace hand pattern on white paper. Cut and glue to the roof of the house to create accumulated snow effect.

With the white paint create mounds of snow and snowflakes to surround the house.

Dilute the glue with water until it appears milky. Paint the hands with this solution. Shake sugar over the glue for a glittery snow effect.

ACTIVITY: Cuddle up to a good story to escape the wintry chill. Three of my favorites are

BOOKS TO ENJOY: *The Snowy Day* by Ezra Jack Keats, 1962, Viking.

Katy and the Big Snow by Virginia Lee Burton, 1943, Houghton Mifflin Co.

Sadie and the Snowman by Allen Morgan, 1987, Scholastic.

GA1079

BULLETIN BOARD:

Background: Use white paper.

Border: bright red paper snow shovels

Attach houses, neighborhood style, and add list of long "o" sounding words.

SHOVEL PATTERN

ACTIVITY:

Make a list of words with the long "o" sound. Print these on a sheet of paper and attach to the bulletin board. This list can keep growing as long as the bulletin board remains a part of the classroom's decoration.

Words that might be included are *row, grow, toe, throw, ghost, gopher, mow,* etc. Students can learn actions for many of these words.

Let's row, row, row our boats.
Let's mow, mow, mow the lawn.
Let's tie a bow, bow, bow on our
    left (right) toe, toe, toe.
Let's tow, tow, tow the wagon full of groceries.

Each time associate the action with the correct word on the list. Eventually pass out slips of paper to the children. On each slip should be a long "o" word. The student can read and do the action and see if classmates can guess the word.

GA1079

Ski Slopes

Anna

MATERIALS: 9" x 12" light-blue paper, 9" x 12" white paper, white paint, crayons and/or construction paper scraps, glue

PROCEDURE: Paint fingers and thumbs of child's hands with white paint. Press upright and slightly extended onto the upper half of the blue paper. Let dry. Cut white paper to form snow line and glue white paper on top of blue paper. With crayons, markers and construction paper, add trees, vehicles, houses, skiers to complete the project.

ACTIVITY: Play appropriate music. Let students do some indoor skiing and ice skating. Yardsticks or cardboard wrapping paper tubes make good ski poles.

BOOKS TO ENJOY: *Cross-Country Cat* by Mary Calhoun, 1979, Morrow.

It's Snowing! It's Snowing! by Jack Prelutsky, 1984, Greenwillow.

GA1079

BULLETIN BOARDS:

Background: shiny silver paper (Christmas wrap or aluminum foil)

Border: Students make snow-flakes or use lace doilies from a variety store.

Attach student ski scenes about the bulletin board area as you wish.

Cut out large paper snowflakes and glue appropriate poems or pictures from magazines.

CREATIVE WRITING:

Have each student complete the following story starter:
In winter I . . . .
glide and slide and float and twirl and twist and turn and fall.
In winter I love to skate.

5

GA1079

Freedom Train

MATERIALS: 9″ x 12″ sheet of black paper, colored construction paper scraps, crayons, scissors, glue, small photo of each child

PROCEDURE: Trace each child's hand (thumb pointed up and fingers to the side and tightly closed). This will be the engine of the train.

From the construction paper scraps, cut out wheels for the engine, other engine features and other train cars.

Glue all pieces to the 9″ x 12″ sheet of black construction paper.

Cut out the small picture of the child and glue it where the engineer sits.

ACTIVITY ONE: Let your students become a "human train." Scatter the children about the classroom or a playground area. Choose one child to be the engine and to chug about and pick up additional cars.

As each child joins the train, he could tell where he would like to go.

A good song to play while the engineer is picking up the cars is "This Train Is Bound for Glory."

ACTIVITY TWO: Discuss the "dreams" of Martin Luther King and how freedom for all people is a goal everyone should work toward.

BOOKS TO ENJOY: *Martin Luther King, Jr.: The Story of a Dream* by June Behrens, 1979, Children's Press.

My First Martin Luther King, Jr. Book by Dee Lillegard, 1987, Children's Press.

BULLETIN BOARD:

Background: blue and white striped denim material for the background

Border: Make railroad tracks from paper or secure toy railroad tracks with straight pins.

Attach freedom trains about the bulletin board area. Add pictures of Martin Luther King and other famous Americans who have contributed to the betterment of all men.

ACTIVITY:

Read *The Little Engine That Could* or a similar story.

Ask each student to tell of a time that he really worked hard to achieve something.

Ask each student to complete the phrase, "If I could, I would _____

_____

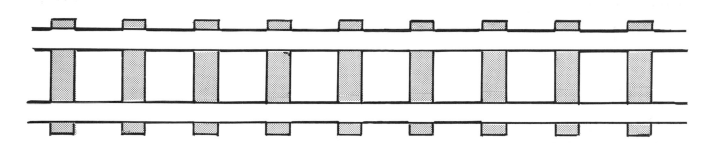

THOUGHT: If you think you can or if you think you can't, you are absolutely right.

Furry Weatherman

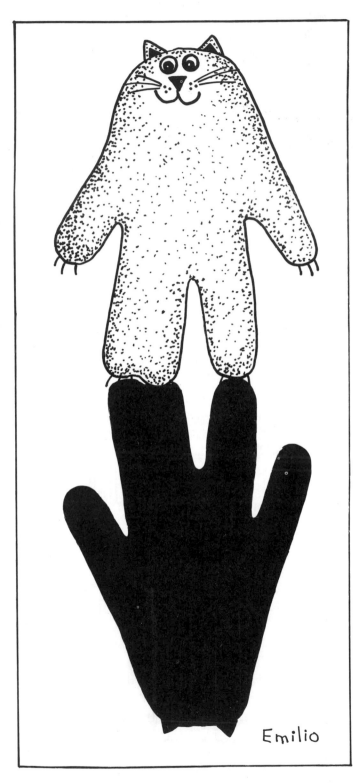

Emilio

MATERIALS:
a piece of white drawing paper for each child, a 5″ x 7″ piece of black construction paper for each child, scissors, crayons, glue

PROCEDURE:
Trace each child's hand on the piece of white drawing paper. The fingers should be extended and the middle and ring fingers should be close together.

Turn paper so fingers are pointing toward the bottom of the paper and have children use crayons to fashion a groundhog.

Trace the child's hand on a piece of black paper to create a shadow for the ground-hog. Cut out the shadow and glue to left or right of the crayon groundhog.

Use crayons to add sun in appropriate position based on position of the shadow. Or have student draw clouds and rain. (No shadows necessary.)

ACTIVITY ONE:
Pair your students and let them pretend to be groundhogs and their shadows. Play a recording of "Me and My Shadow" or another appropriate song as students move about. Occasionally say "Switch" so each child gets a turn being the shadow.

ACTIVITY TWO:
A second fun activity is to shine a flashlight or bright desk lamp on a white wall or large sheet of paper. Invite students to create "lamp puppets."

BOOKS TO ENJOY:
It's Groundhog Day! by Steven Kroll, 1987, Holiday.

Groundhog's Day at the Doctor by Judy Delton, 1981, Parents.

WARNING: Be sure to complete the activity on the next page before having the children create the picture.

BULLETIN BOARD:
Background: gray paper or newspaper that includes weather maps and information

Border: large black construction paper question marks

Place finished groundhogs (with or without shadows) about the board.

ACTIVITY:
Discuss placement of the sun and the shadow. Take the children outside on a sunny day. In the morning use chalk to print child's name on blacktop or concrete area. Use chalk to draw the shadow. Return outdoors in the afternoon. Have the child stand in the same place and draw the afternoon shadow. Discuss.

Some vocabulary words to include with this lesson are

| winter | spring | shadow | morning |
| afternoon | forecast | weather | predict |

GA1079

Woven Love

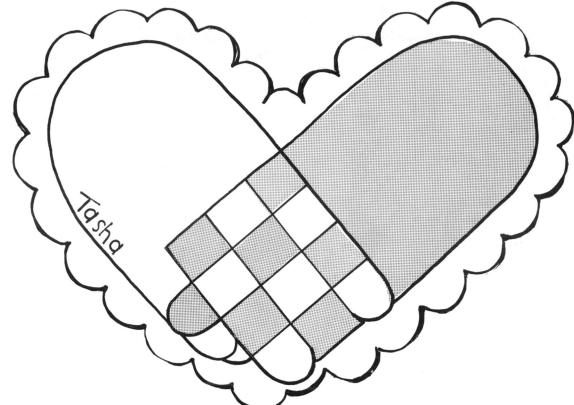

MATERIALS: two 5″ x 7″ sheets of colored paper (red, purple, pink), one scalloped heart shape cut from a sheet of 9″ x 12″ white construction paper, scissors, glue

PROCEDURE: Ask each student to choose two colors of the 5″ x 7″ paper.

Trace and cut out a hand from each sheet; omit the thumbs.

Slit the fingers and begin weaving the fingers as you would in normal paper weaving.

Secure ends with dabs of glue. Glue woven heart to large scalloped white heart.

ACTIVITY: Play some games to celebrate Valentine's Day in your classroom.

a. Preschoool and kindergarten children will enjoy A Tisket, a Tasket. Instead of dropping a note, have the player who is "it" drop a bright red heart-shaped piece of paper.

b. Primary students might enjoy a Heart Toss game. Place some large hearts on the floor. Use tape to secure the position of each heart. Place a different number on each heart. Players stand behind a line and toss tiny candy hearts onto the bigger hearts. Points can be added. No matter what the score, let every child be a winner. Save some candy hearts and let each child enjoy a few.

BOOKS TO ENJOY: *The Valentine Star* by Patricia R. Giff, 1985, Dell.

Miss Flora McFlimsey's Valentine by Mariana, 1987, Lothrop.

GA1079

BULLETIN BOARD:

Background: Use pink paper or sheets of a small print valentine designed wrapping paper.

Border: Use lace or eyelet trim from a fabric store for a border. Save this for future use. It will make a nice border in the spring as well as for a December or January bulletin board.

In the center of the bulletin board area, place a large red heart. On it print *Be Mine* or another candy heart valentine saying. Attach the student-completed hearts about the bulletin board area. Commercially made valentines could be added to complete the display.

ACTIVITY:

Do a little giggling today. Have the children sit in a circle and in turn complete phrases like the following examples:
I don't like _____ on my hamburger.
I don't like _____ on my pizza.
Never, never, never try to catch a _____.
I saw a lady wearing _____ in her hair.
   umbrellas
   cucumbers
   purple socks
   yesterday's newspaper
   Play-Doh
Never, never, never stuff a _____ in your pocket.

GA1079

Long Abe Lincoln

MATERIALS:

white drawing paper for making 2½" circles (one for each child), large sheets of black construction paper (12" x 18"), crayons, scissors, glue

PROCEDURE:

Place child's hand and arm on sheet of black construction paper. Trace and cut out. Turn so fingers point to bottom and form Abe's beard.

Glue 2½" white paper circle in center of hand (beard) area. Children draw Abe's honest face on the circle, using crayons.

From scraps of black construction paper, cut out strip of paper to form brim of Abe's hat. Glue in appropriate place.

Each child now has his very own Abraham Lincoln with a very long stovepipe hat.

OPTIONAL:

Strips of black yarn can be glued to the face to make a fuzzy beard and/or hair.

ACTIVITY:

Share the story of Abraham Lincoln's boyhood and life with your students. An excellent book is *Abraham Lincoln* by Ingri and Edgar d' Aulaire.

Make large paper stovepipe hats for your students to wear. It should be easy to pretend about being the sixteenth President with these hats firmly in place.

Discuss the term *honesty*. Why is honesty the best policy? Ask the children to tell of a time when they were honest. What was the result of that honesty?

Discuss the results of being dishonest. Ask the children to tell of a time they were not honest. What were the results?

BOOKS TO ENJOY:

Abraham Lincoln by Ingri and Edgar d' Aulaire, 1987, Doubleday.

If You Grew up with Abraham Lincoln by Ruth Gross, 1985, Scholastic.

Lincoln's Birthday by Clyde Bulla, 1966, Harper Jr. Books.

Jenny

12

BULLETIN BOARD:

Background: white paper

Border: red, white and blue crepe paper streamers

Attach completed Abe Lincolns to the bulletin board area.

ACTIVITY:

Glue pieces of lined paper to Abe's hat. These should be slightly smaller than the hat so a black border can be seen. On the paper list things that can be found or worn on the head. Hair, eye, nose, ear, chin, cap, hat, bow, wig and hair net are just a few.

An alternative would be for each child to list additional positive characteristics of a leader or friend. These can be printed on the lined paper for the child.

 GA1079

Truthful Tree

MATERIALS:
red and green paint
9" x 12" white drawing paper
brown crayon

PROCEDURE:
Paint each child's hand green and press it on the sheet of drawing paper. With the brown crayon make a tree trunk.

Dip the tip of the child's index finger in red paint to add cherries to the tree.

ACTIVITY:
Re-create the tale about George Washington and the cherry tree by playing Pin the Hatchet on the Tree. The rules are the same as in Pin the Tail on the Donkey.

You will need a poster with a large cherry tree drawn on it, a blindfold and a paper hatchet for each child. You will find a hatchet pattern on the next page.

BOOKS TO ENJOY:
George Washington by Ingri and Edgar d' Aulaire, 1987, Doubleday.

My First Presidents' Day Book by Aileen Fisher, 1987, Children's Press.

If You Grew up with George Washington by Ann McGovern, 1985, Scholastic.

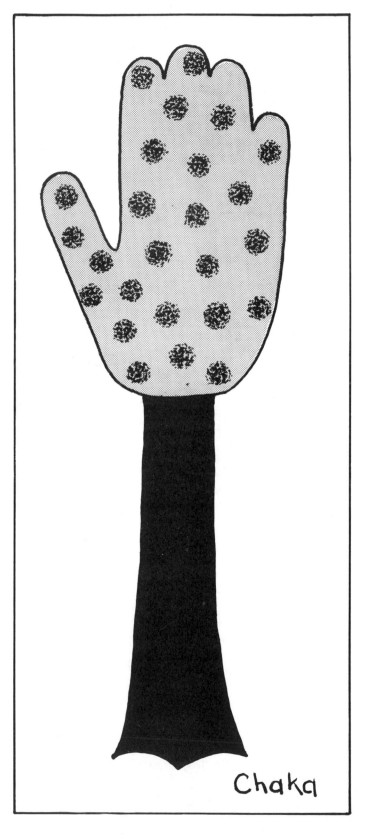
Chaka

GA1079

TWO BULLETIN BOARD IDEAS

Arrange completed student trees about the bulletin board area in an orchard fashion. Find pictures of things that grow on trees in magazines. Cut out appropriate pictures and glue or tack to the bulletin board area. The names of the things that grow on trees can also be printed about the bulletin board area.

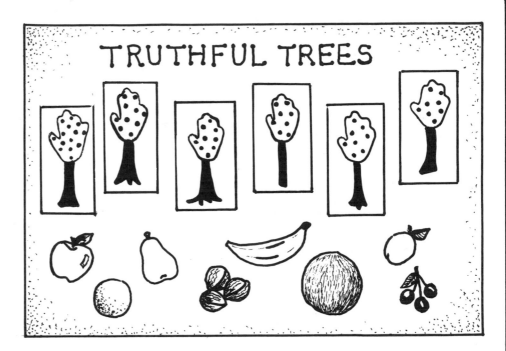

Trace each child's hand on a piece of green construction paper. Cut hands out and arrange to form one large tree. Add a construction paper trunk and bright red construction paper cherries. Trim the bulletin board area with strips of scalloped red paper. Have each child print his name on his hand. This can be used for the game Pin the Hatchet on the Tree.

Here is a handy hatchet pattern for the Pin the Hatchet on the Tree game. Cut hatchets from stiff paper (index cards or railroad board) and cover blade area with tinfoil.

HATCHET PATTERN

GA1079

Winter's Last Roar

Andrew

curl

MATERIALS:	yellow and brown paint, white drawing paper, crayons, scissors, pencil
OPTIONAL:	You may wish to make the lion's whiskers from pipe cleaners or yarn. Cut appropriate length and glue in place.
PROCEDURE:	Paint both of the child's hands yellow. Make first print with hands together at thumbs and with the fingers extended. Make second print with the hands together omitting thumbs. Allow print to dry.
	When dry, use brown paint to create the lion's facial features.
	Cut out entire print and curl the lion's mane by rolling each finger around a pencil.
ACTIVITY:	Have a weather watch during the month of March. Does the month really enter like a lion and exit like a lamb? Make a chart and record each day's weather.
BOOKS TO ENJOY:	*Hungry as a Lion* by Marilyn Anderson, 1985, Willowisp Press.
	Dandelion by Don Freeman, 1964, Viking.
	Snow Lion by David McPhail, 1983, Parents.

GA1079

SAMPLE WEATHER CHART

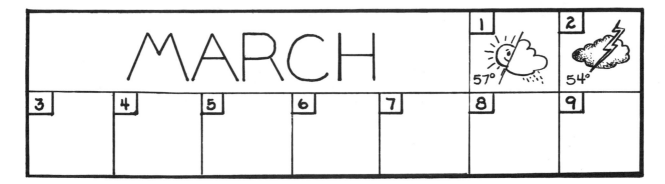

BULLETIN BOARD:

Background: gray paper or sheets of the newspaper that include weather information

Border: Paint small twigs green and glue to form the border. The pussy willows can be made by dipping fingertips in paint and making prints.

Attach completed student work.

ACTIVITY:

Have fun by making a variety of animal sounds. Students will enjoy being creative with their voices. Let the students use their voices to distinguish between a baby and adult animal.

Play "Carnival of the Animals" by Saint Seins. Allow students to identify the various animals as the music plays. This is an excellent time to add some creative animal movements.

GA1079

Lucky Leprechaun

MATERIALS:
orange and green paint, 5" x 7" piece of pink paper, crayons, scissors

OPTIONAL:
one green ball fringe for each child

PROCEDURE:
Paint thumb and heel of each child's hand green.

Leave center of palm unpainted.

Paint fingers of child's hand orange.

Leave center of palm unpainted.

Press painted hand onto pink paper and let dry.

Use crayons to create an elfish leprechaun face.

Cut out and curl fingers for a fanciful Irish fellow.

OPTIONAL:
Glue green ball of fringe to tip of thumb to add tassel for the hat.

ACTIVITY: Play a relay game to celebrate Saint Patrick's Day. Divide your students into two teams. Turn your class trash can into a "pot of gold" and place it on one side of the classroom.

Have each child place one candy gold coin on his "Lucky Leprechaun" face and race in turn to put the candy coin in the "pot of gold." If the child drops his gold coin when enroute to the "pot of gold," he must either count to 10 before continuing or return and begin again from the starting place.

Your students will have great fun trying to be as quick as those little Irish sprites. Of course there are no losers. Everyone gets to have some of the candy.

TIPS: If gold wrapped coin candy is difficult to find, simply wrap peppermints in gold foil.

Use a yellow marker to make a "Pot of Gold" sign for the trash can.

BOOKS TO ENJOY: *St. Patrick's Day* by Joyce Kessell, 1982, Carolrhoda Books.

Leprechauns Never Lie by Lorna Balian, 1980, Abingdon.

Leprechaun's Story by Richard Kennedy, 1979, Dutton.

18

GA1079

LUCKY LEPRECHAUNS

BODY PATTERN

BULLETIN BOARD:

Background: On a white sheet of paper create a class-painted mural. Included should be a giant rainbow, a pot of gold and several trees.

Border: One is not needed, but green construction paper shamrocks could be made.

On the right is a pattern for the body of a leprechaun. Cut from white paper and allow each child to color. Glue head and face to body and place on the bulletin board area.

GA1079

Freckled Frog

MATERIALS:

5″ x 7″ sheet of light-green paper, green paint, crayons, scissors, large sheet of green paper, white paper

PROCEDURE:

Paint each child's hand green and press it on the piece of light-green paper. Let dry.

Add frog features with crayons or markers. Two frog eyes should be added to the heel of the child's hand.

OPTIONAL:

Glue two "goo-goo" eyes to the frog instead of making paper ones. These can be found at most craft stores.

ACTIVITY ONE:

Play leap frog in relay race fashion. Make up teams of players. Each team should have four to six players. All teams begin leaping at the same time and the first to a designated spot wins.

Tape a large green lily pad to the center of the play area. This can easily be made from a piece of green poster board.

ACTIVITY TWO:

Make several small lily pads. Tape each to the floor of the playing area. Keeping legs together, the children try to hop from pad to pad. Increase difficulty by placing pads farther and farther apart.

The pads could be numbered or lettered in sequential order and the children could count or recite the letters of the alphabet as they hop.

ACTIVITY THREE:

The teacher is the leader and mommy or daddy frog. The children are standing at random behind the leader. The leader says, "hop forward," "hop left," "hop right," "hop sideways," etc. All the little frogs follow directions.

BOOKS TO ENJOY:

Frog Went A-Courting by Nina Barbaresi, 1985, Scholastic.

Days with Frog and Toad by Arnold Lobel, 1984, Harper Jr.

Frog on His Own by Mercer Mayer, 1980, Dial Books.

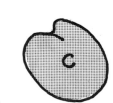

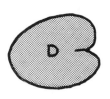

GA1079

SPRING FROLIC

BULLETIN BOARD:	Background: light-blue paper
	Border: wavy design of darker blue, on the bottom only
	Attach frogs on lily pads about the bulletin board area.
	Add various colors of flowers. (Patterns below.)
ACTIVITY ONE:	Green signifies growth and that means spring. Brainstorm with your children. Make a list of things that are green. Create another smaller bulletin board and cover it completely with things that are green.
ACTIVITY TWO:	Frogs can be found around a pond. If you live in a geographical area where there are ponds, visit one. What other forms of living plants and animals can you find in your investigation?

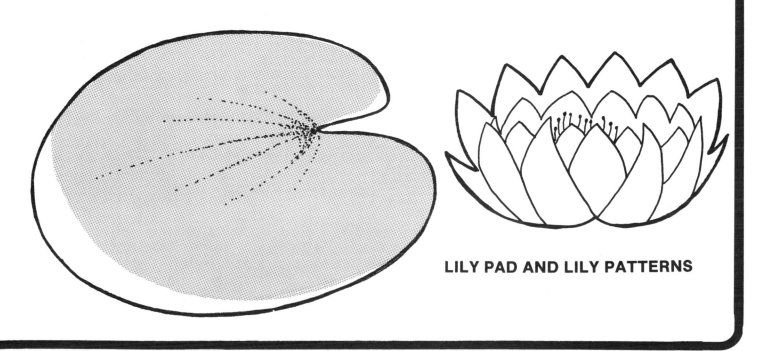

LILY PAD AND LILY PATTERNS

GA1079

Out Like a Lamb

B.J.

MATERIALS: 5″ x 7″ white drawing paper, black and white paint, glue, cotton balls

PROCEDURE: Paint hand and middle three fingers black.

Paint thumb and little finger white.

Press on drawing paper. Let dry.

Add construction paper or "goo-goo" eyes.

Cover ears with glue and add wisps of fluffy white cotton.

ACTIVITY: Tell the class a springtime story using a "woolly" tool to help you. Ahead of time, roll a large ball of yarn from several long pieces of different colored yarn.

Assemble your students in a circle and begin telling your story about spring.

Each student adds a portion of the story while unrolling the ball of yarn. A turn is up when the color of the yarn changes.

Continue the storytelling around the circle until everyone has had a turn. Remember to mention in your part of the story that an old saying is that if March comes in like a lion, it goes out like a lamb.

Preschoolers may need to have a variation in this activity. The pieces of woolly yarn should be much shorter, and possibly the students should be asked for just a few words, not sentences, during turns. You may adapt to your own situation. A list of springtime books is on the next page.

GA1079

BULLETIN BOARD:

Background: grey wool fabric, felt would be OK

Border: cotton batting trim or glue fluffy cotton balls to various colors of construction paper

Scatter lambs about the bulletin board area. In the open areas place pictures found in magazines of other baby animals.

In a pocket in one of the lower corners of the bulletin board, place strips of paper. On one strip should be the adult name of an animal. On the other should be the name of the baby animal—cow, calf; sheep, lamb, etc.

For older children you may wish to use male/female/baby combinations. Ram, ewe, lamb, etc. To complete this activity, students would group the three appropriate strips.

SPRING BOOKS:

My Little Lamb by Patricia Crampton, 1987, Bradbury Press.

First Day of Spring by Sharon Gordon, 1981, Troll Assoc.

I Love Spring by Steven Kroll, 1987, Holiday.

GA1079

Umbrella Days

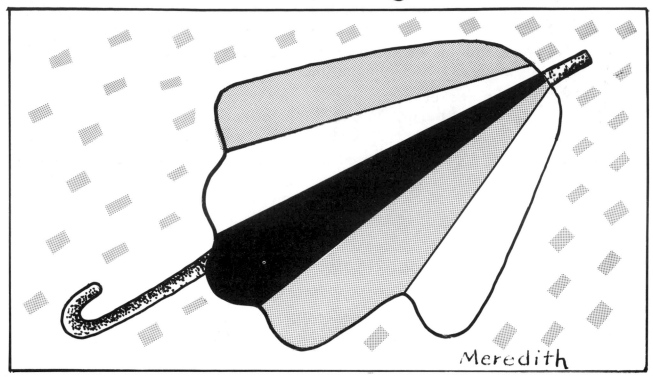

Meredith

MATERIALS: 5" x 7" pieces of paper, assorted colors; pipe cleaners; Q-tips; crayons; glue; blue paint; 9" x 12" sheets of blue or gray paper

PROCEDURE: Trace hand on 5" x 7" piece of paper.

Section off each finger by drawing a line back to the heel of the hand. Choose two colors and let the student color the five strips alternately.

Turn hand upside down and place on large sheet of paper at a slight angle.

Before gluing the hand to the larger sheet of paper, put a pipe cleaner under it. Bend to form tip and handle. Glue the hand in place.

Dip Q-tips in blue paint and spot rain all over the paper. Now the artwork is sure to "drip" with success.

ACTIVITY: Play a rainy day game by tossing raindrops (beanbags) into an upside down umbrella.

Cut ten pieces of construction paper to resemble raindrops. Number them one through ten. Tape these to the play area at various distances from the umbrella. All children line up on number one. When a successful toss has been made, the student moves to raindrop number two and continues in turn until ten successful tosses have been made.

So that no child will feel he is a loser, you play also. Simply miss as often as necessary so some child does not remain alone on number six while all others are on number ten.

BOOKS TO ENJOY: *Taste the Raindrops* by Anna G. Hines, 1983, Greenwillow.

Peter Spier's Rain by Peter Spier, 1982, Doubleday.

GA1079

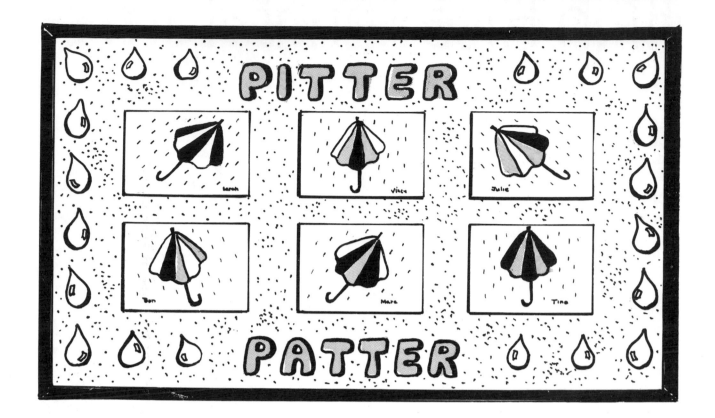

BULLETIN BOARD:

Background: light-blue paper splatter painted with dark-blue paint

Border: silver paper raindrops or tiny paper umbrellas (available at party supply stores)

Place completed umbrella pictures about the bulletin board area. You may wish to add pictures of puddles, ponds, rivers, lakes and even oceans. Label each body of water with the appropriate name.

ACTIVITY ONE:

Lead a class discussion. Topics can range from "What do we wear to protect us from the rain?" to "How do we protect ourselves from other types of weather?" Be sure to point out that barns protect animals from weather and houses protect people from weather.

ACTIVITY TWO:

Discuss the good and bad aspects of a rain. Too much rain and we have a flood. What are some things to do inside on days when it is rainy and gloomy? Crops need rain to grow and produce food. In some areas of the world they have very destructive forms of rain, such as hurricanes, typhoons, tornadoes, hail, sleet, blizzards.

GA1079

High Rise Inhabitants

Lincoln

MATERIALS:

8½" x 11" piece of white paper, brown construction paper, various colors of yarn scraps, crayons, glue

PROCEDURE:

From the brown construction paper, make a tree trunk similar to the one shown at the right. Glue to the sheet of white paper.

Place fingers on the horizontal branch of the tree and trace the fingers to form the shape for five baby birds.

Color birds desired color(s) and add features with crayons. Bits of yarn can be glued to create head feathers.

Glue various colors of yarn scraps to the picture to create a nest.

ACTIVITY ONE:

Invite your students to become feathered fellows of spring. Play the circle game Bluebird, Bluebird Through My Window. Words and music can be found in the book *Sally Go Round the Sun* by Edith Fowke.

ACTIVITY TWO:

This is a good project to correlate with a study of various homes. Of course a study of the types of homes that animals live in would be appropriate.

Sometimes young children do not realize that peers in other locations live in homes much different from theirs. Collect pictures of a variety of types of dwellings and allow the children to discuss how life would be different in a condo or a ranch house, etc.

BOOKS TO ENJOY:

Are You My Mother? by Phillip Eastman, 1967, Random House Beginner Books.

Georgie and the Baby Birds by Robert Bright, 1983, Doubleday.

GA1079

BULLETIN BOARD: Background: dark blue or green paper

Border: real feathers, purchased from a craft store

Place completed student pictures about the bulletin board area and add pictures of animal homes. Then replace the animal homes with the various types of dwellings in which humans live.

ACTIVITY: Borrow the feathers from the bulletin board and have some feather fun. Encourage each child to blow a feather and see how long it can be kept afloat. Have each child blow the feather in the air and then try to catch it in his palm, then on the back of his hand, then on his elbow, then on his knee and finally on his foot.

Pair the children and repeat the process. One child blows the feather while the other child makes the appropriate catch.

GA1079

Bunny Hop

Mandy

MATERIALS: 5" x 7" piece of paper (white, gray, brown or black), cotton balls, glue, scissors

PROCEDURE: Trace each child's hand. Turn the hand horizontally. The thumb and index fingers should be extended up while the other fingers are held together. If the child has trouble controlling fingers, use a rubber band or length of yarn to hold fingers together.

Use pink, blue and black crayons to add the bunny's features.

Glue cotton on the handprint to create a fluffy tail.

ACTIVITY: Teach your students how to do the Bunny Hop. Music and directions may be found on the Melody House record *Hokey Pokey,* etc.

Older students may enjoy making and wearing bunny ears while bunny hopping about the room.

BOOKS TO ENJOY: *The Easter Bunny That Overslept* by Priscilla and Otto Friedrich, 1983, Lothrop.

The Big Bunny and the Easter Eggs by Steven Kroll, 1982, Holiday.

The Easter Bunny by Winfried Wolf, 1986, Dial Books Young.

Use this carrot pattern to create an alternative border for your bulletin board.

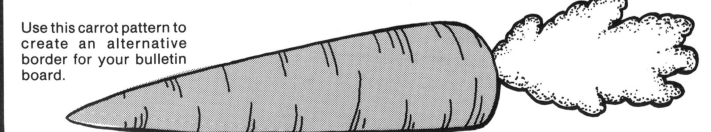

CARROT PATTERN

GA1079

BULLETIN BOARD:

Background: blue paper

Border: Attach commercial Easter grass across the bottom of the bulletin board area. Construction paper tulips can be made for the two sides.

Fasten bunnies about the bulletin board area.

ACTIVITY:

All children love action, and a hippity-hop bunny seems to be the perfect introduction for some action.

Print a series of action words on 8½" x 11" pieces of paper. Words could include:

hop	jump	skip	tiptoe
slide	stand	flap	turn
spin	smile	shake	wiggle

Shuffle these cards and hold one up and get ready for action. In a few seconds hold up another card. Continue through several actions. The final card should say "Sit."

hop	shake arms	wiggle toes
shake hands	turn	tiptoe

Peeking Out

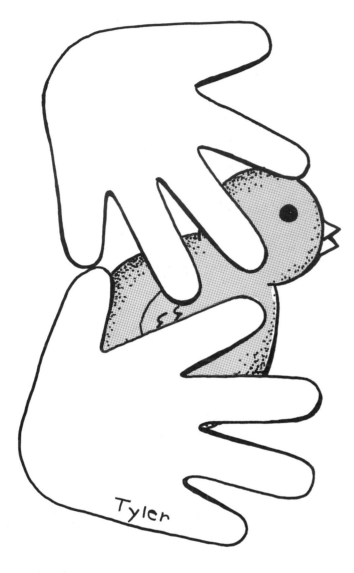

Tyler

MATERIALS:
two 5″ x 7″ sheets of white drawing paper, yellow paper, scissors, glue, crayons

PROCEDURE:
On the sheets of white drawing paper, trace both hands of each student in your class.

Outline each hand with a black crayon or liquid marker.

Cut out hands.

Use the pattern below to make a "chick" for each child's picture.

Use crayons to make beak orange and eye blue, or create these features from orange and blue construction paper and glue to the chick pattern.

Reverse one of the hand patterns so one thumb is touching the baby finger of the other hand; then glue the chick in the appropriate position.

ACTIVITY:
Begin a study about egg hatching. Read books, watch a film or, best of all, borrow an incubator and hatch your own eggs. A field trip to a farm or hatchery would be an added bonus if you live in a rural area. Those of you who live in an urban area may also be able to find a nearby museum.

BOOKS TO ENJOY:
A Chick Hatches by Joanna Cole, 1976, Morrow.

Little Chick's Big Day by Mary Kwitz, 1981, Harper Jr.

CHICK PATTERN

30

GA1079

BULLETIN BOARD: Background: blue paper

Border: real eggshells cracked and glued to the background paper

Place completed student projects about the bulletin board area. Add student writing.

WRITING ACTIVITY: Through a film or by actual viewing, the students will realize that a baby chick will make several noises and movements. These sounds and actions can be turned into student-created writings.

Peep! Peep!
I see you.
Do you see me?
Peep! Peep!
I hear you.
Do you hear me?

Peep, peep, peep
Peck, peck, peck
Poke, poke, poke,
Peep, peck, poke.
Here I am!

Help your group of children to listen and hear and discover many ideas. Then allow each child to dictate a poem or story to you. Mount completed effort on a bright orange piece of construction paper and attach to the bulletin board area.

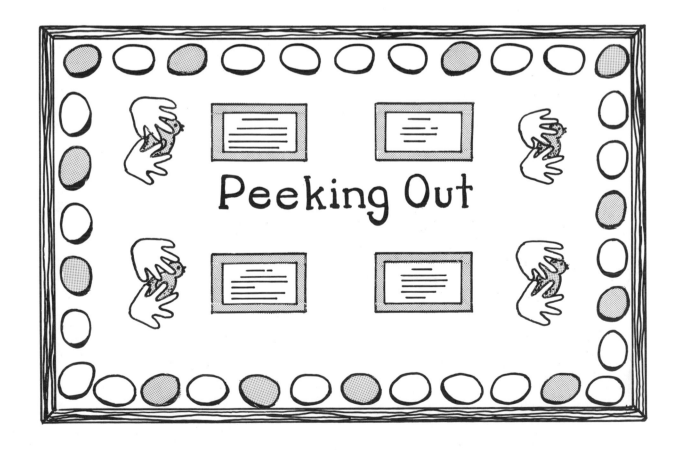

GA1079

May Day Hooray

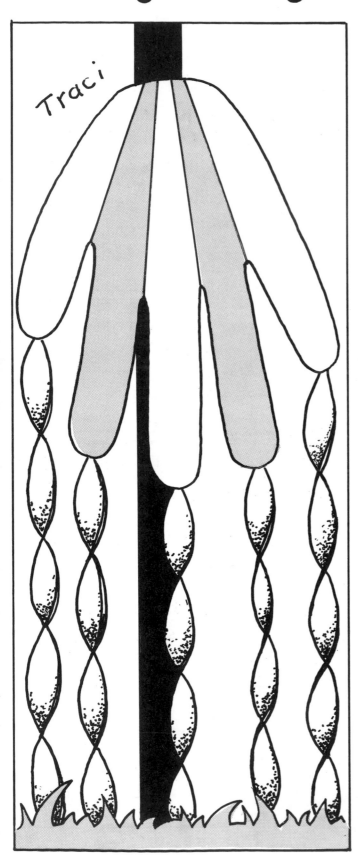

Traci

MATERIALS:
pink, yellow, light green, light blue and lavender paints; 9" x 12" sheet of paper cut in half vertically (light blue); crepe paper streamers in the same colors as the paints; glue; scissors; crayons

PROCEDURE:
Paint each finger of the child's hand a different pastel color. Begin at the base of the palm and continue to the fingertip.

Place hand about two inches from the top of the piece of blue paper, fingers pointing down, and press hard.

Glue crepe paper strips to the fingertips and twist before securing to the bottom. Be careful and use just a dab of glue.

Black paint, a strip of black construction paper or a thick black pipe cleaner could be used to create the pole.

ACTIVITY:
Teach your class the Maypole dance. Directions may be found in the book *Special Holidays Handbook*, Children's Press, 1986.

BOOKS TO ENJOY:
Miss Flora McFlimsey's May Day by Mariana, 1987, Lothrop.

Spring and May by Nancy Davis, 1986, DaNa Publications.

GA1079

BULLETIN BOARD:

Background: a bright sunny yellow paper or floral wrapping paper (small print)

Border: large paper flowers crafted from a variety of colors of construction paper

Attach student Maypoles about the bulletin board area. Listed below are suggestions for several ways to complete this May bulletin board.

a. Cut pictures of springtime scenes from old magazines and add to the area.

b. Cut pictures of people of all ages from old magazines. The people should be enjoying springtime activities.

c. Add pictures of springtime flowers to the bulletin board area. Greeting cards and old garden catalogs are a good source for pictures of flowers.

d. Display a sampling of each child's printing. Let each child tell you some words that rhyme with *May*. Print the list of words for the child to copy. Mount the word lists on pieces of green construction paper.

33

Handy Bouquet

MATERIALS:

red, pink, yellow or lavender paint; 9" x 12" sheet of blue paper; crayons; craft ribbon (optional)

PROCEDURE:

Paint each child's hand the color of his choice.

Press to make handprint near the top of the blue piece of paper. Fingers should be together and pointed upward.

Make a stem and leaves by coloring or cut from pieces of green construction paper and glue to the background paper.

OPTIONAL:

Cut stem and leaves from pieces of craft ribbon and glue.

Now each child has created a very special blossom for Mom.

ACTIVITY:

Have your students use their hands in another special way. Plant flower seeds in half-pint milk cartons.

Before filling the cartons with potting soil, cover the outside with a bright patterned piece of Con-Tact paper.

Place planted seeds in a sunny window. Water daily and provide much tender loving care.

The progress of the plant growth can be carefully watched, discussed and recorded by having children draw weekly pictures.

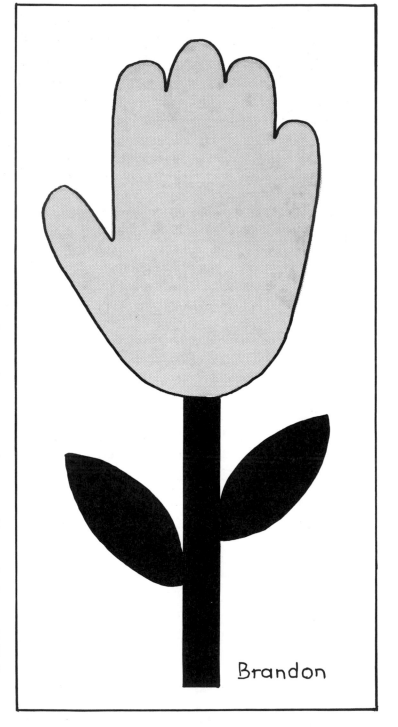

Brandon

BOOKS TO ENJOY:

Something for Mom by Norma Sawicki, 1987, Lothrop.

Hooray for Mothers' Day! by Marjorie Sharmat, 1986, Holiday.

GA1079

**BULLETIN
BOARD:**

Background: blue paper on the top two-thirds of the board area and green paper on the bottom one-third

Border: None is necessary. A bright smiling sun and a couple of fluffy white clouds could be placed in the sky of the bulletin board area.

Cut out student-made flowers and plant them about the bulletin board area. Add student poems to complete the garden setting.

ACTIVITY:

Isn't it funny how moms know just what it takes to make little children smile? Brainstorm with your students the nice things that moms do.

Plug each child's responses into the poem model below, and you will have an A+ Mother's Day gift to send home.

Completed poems can become part of the bulletin board.

Moms know how little kids grow ....(given)

on hugs and kisses all day long } (student)
on lots of macaroni and cheese } input)
on trips to the park on sunny days }

Moms are smart when it comes to kids.......................(given)

GA1079

Spring Serenade

Noah

MATERIALS: blue paper cut 18″ wide and 6″ high; brown construction paper for tree branch; yellow, blue or red construction paper for bird; brown and green paint; crayons; glue

OPTIONAL: green fabric scraps for leaves, blue and orange construction paper for eye and beak

PROCEDURE: Glue construction paper branch and bird to blue paper.

Paint both hands of each child brown. Omit thumbs.

Press painted hands firmly on paper in appropriate position to create a nest.

Add details to bird and leaves to branch.

ACTIVITY: Take your class on a springtime discovery walk. Point out and list everything seen that signifies spring.

GA1079

BULLETIN BOARD:

Background: brown or tan paper or burlap material

Border: light green paper leaves

Attach completed student work about the bulletin board area. Recall your springtime discovery walk and ask children what some of the signs of spring were. Print these words on index cards and add to the bulletin board.

BOOKS TO ENJOY:

The Nightingale by Hans Christian Andersen, 1984, Picture Book Studio.

Birdsong by Gail Haley, 1984, Crown Books.

PATTERNS

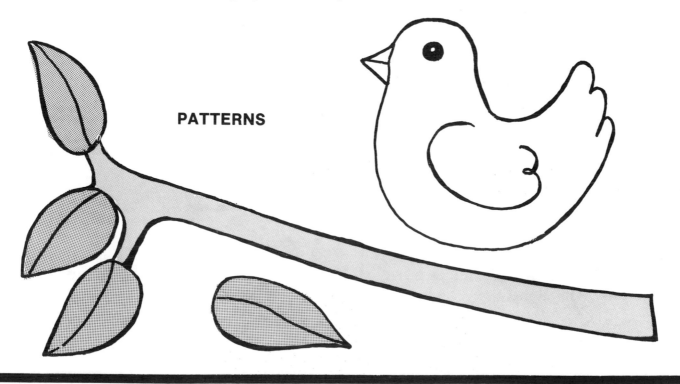

Scoops of Spring

MATERIALS:

5" x 7" pieces of ice-cream colored paper, pieces of burlap material cut in cone shapes, glue, marker, pencil, wallpaper samples for background

PROCEDURE:

Trace both of each child's hands. Omit the thumbs. Allow each child to choose what flavor (color of paper) of ice cream he would like.

Cut out the hands and trim bottom to a "V" shape so cone will cover.

Glue the handy scoop of ice cream to the piece of wallpaper.

Cut a piece of burlap in an ice-cream cone shape and glue in appropriate position.

ACTIVITY ONE:

Borrow an ice-cream maker and demonstrate how ice cream is made. Let all students help with the cooking and cranking.

ACTIVITY TWO:

Make a list of ice-cream flavors. Let each child tell which is his favorite. When all have had a turn, tell them your favorite is peanut butter, marshmallow ripple or cornflake crunch or fudge pizza pecan. Encourage all students to invent some new flavors. Have fun laughing and imagining the taste of the fun-filled flavors suggested.

BOOKS TO ENJOY:

From Milk to Ice Cream by Ali Mitgutsch, 1981, Carolrhoda Books.

Touch of Spring by Viola Smith, 1976, LeNape Publishing.

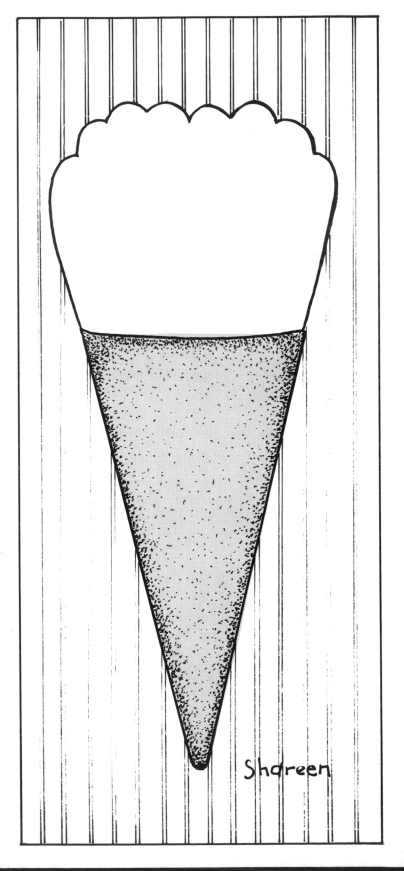

Shareen

GA1079

BULLETIN BOARD:

Background: paper bags or place mats purchased at various ice cream businesses in your area, . . . logos showing

Border: spoons, napkins, straws, etc., from the same establishments

Attach student-made ice-cream cones. Print the names of the imaginative flavors from activity two on index cards or similar-sized pieces of construction paper.

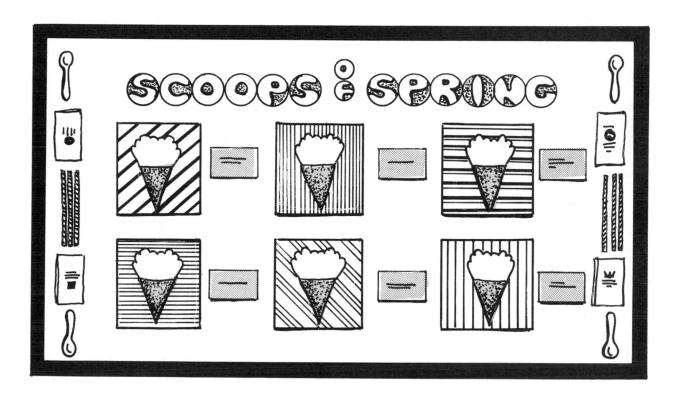

ACTIVITY ONE:

Remember the old rhyme, "I scream! You scream! We all scream for ice cream"? Try this variation. I scream! You scream! We all scream for _____ ice cream. Each student can decide what imaginative flavor he would like to include in the rhyme. Student-printed copies can be mounted on construction paper and placed by the student's ice-cream cone.

ACTIVITY TWO:

Play a memory game. Gather students in a circle. One student starts by saying, "I like vanilla ice cream." The student to the left says, "I like vanilla and pecan ice cream." The third student says, "I like vanilla, pecan and chocolate ice cream." The process continues around the circle. The list just keeps on growing. A second time choose another student to begin.

GA1079

Bow Tie Guy

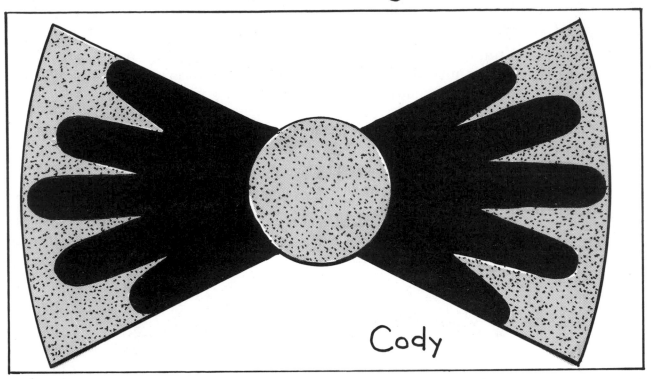

Cody

MATERIALS: red, navy, brown, green or black paint; material scraps at least 8" x 10" in size; tie boxes from a department store or white poster board cut to tie box size; scissors; glue

PROCEDURE: Cut large bow tie-shaped pieces from the scraps of material.

For each bow tie shape also cut one 2" to 2½" circle from the same material.

Glue bow tie shape onto the tie box and let dry. Do not glue the circle at this time.

Paint both hands of each student a color to coordinate with the tie fabric and press hard to print on top of the fabric as shown in the example. Again allow time for drying.

Glue circle of material where palms meet. Glue entire tie to the top of the box or the piece of white poster board.

This is one tie that definitely won't be returnable this Father's Day.

ACTIVITY: Fold an 8½" x 11" piece of white paper to create a greeting card. Children can use crayons or markers to design the cover. Older children can also create the inside message. For younger children, print the special message of their choice for them. Of course a personalized signature will be needed.

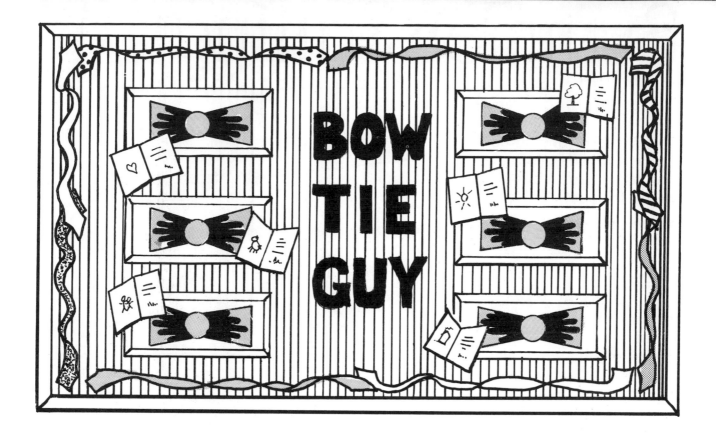

BULLETIN BOARD:	Background: Father's Day gift wrap paper or striped wallpaper—plain brown wrapping paper would be a third alternative
	Border: old ties stapled in a looped fashion
	There will be several dads who will donate "special" ties they have received as gifts.
	Place completed student artwork and greeting cards about the bulletin board area.
	An extra touch that could be added would be pictures of fathers interacting with children.
ACTIVITY:	This would be a great time to have the children practice tying a bow. Wrap a few empty boxes of various sizes with brightly colored gift wrap. Provide various types of material for tying bows (string, yarn, ribbon, etc.) and allow time for the children to tie bows on the packages.
BOOKS TO ENJOY:	*Daddy Makes the Best Spaghetti* by Anna Hines, 1986, Clarion.
	Just Me and My Dad by Mercer Mayer, 1977, Western Publishing.

GA1079

Summer Sailing

MATERIALS:

5" x 7" pieces of colored construction paper (could be larger), brown paper for boat, 9" x 12" piece of blue paper, crayons, markers, glue, scissors

PROCEDURE:

On a piece of 5" x 7" paper, trace the child's hand. The thumb should be extended while the fingers are held closely together.

Using crayons or markers, add a design to the sail and cut it out.

On the sheet of blue paper, glue a boat and mast that have been cut from brown paper.

With a black marker outline the ship's flag.

Glue the "handy" sail in the appropriate place to complete the picture.

Now you are off and sailing if the breezes are favorable.

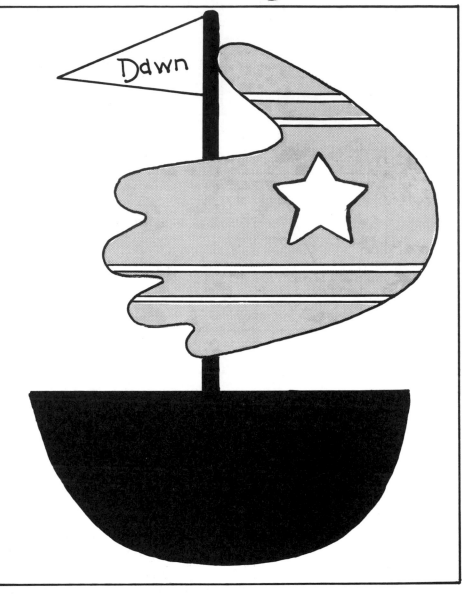

ACTIVITY:

Make some mini sailboats and test sail them. You will need half a walnut shell, some gum or Silly Putty, a toothpick and a small sail made of paper.

Clean the inside of the walnut shell. Chew the gum to soften and press some inside the hollow shell. Stick in the toothpick and use the toothpick to poke two holes in the paper sail to hold in place.

Fill a plastic wading pool with water and set the sailboats afloat. Some adjustments will need to be made in the sails for balance. When all the boats are afloat, have the children circle the pool and provide wind by blowing gently.

42

GA1079

BULLETIN BOARD:	Background: Use white paper and create a sky and sea mural painted by the students.
	Border: paper waves
	Attach student-made sailboats and use a blue marker to add a few final waves.
ACTIVITY:	Ask students who have been aboard a boat of any kind to share their experiences with classmates.
	Ask students where they would like to sail. Hawaii! Around the world! Show pictures from travel magazines.
	Discuss boat safety. Using the tiny walnut sailboats made by the students, demonstrate how dangerous a boat can be.
BOOKS TO ENJOY:	*The Maggie B.* by Irene Haas, 1975, Macmillan.
	Sailing with the Wind by Thomas Locker, 1986, Dial Books Young.

GA1079

Growing Season

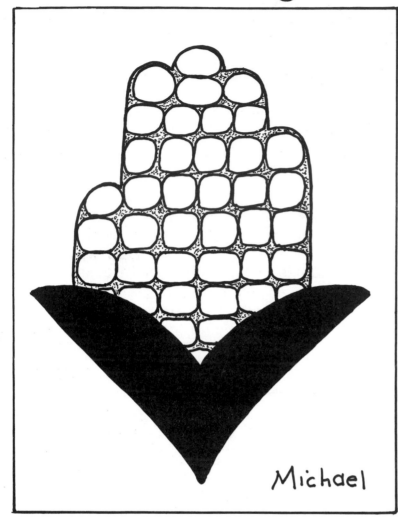

Michael

MATERIALS:

5" x 7" piece of yellow paper, green paper cut to resemble corn husks, crayons, scissors, glue

PROCEDURE:

Trace the outline of each child's hand on yellow paper. Make sure all fingers are held closely together while tracing is done.

Use yellow crayon to make rows of yellow corn. Cover entire hand area.

Glue husks to the corn.

OPTIONAL:

Older students may enjoy using a paper punch to make yellow circles. These can be glued in rows to the outline of the hand to form the kernels.

ACTIVITY:

Plant a small vegetable garden. Window boxes could be used. You might consider converting a plastic swimming pool or an old sandbox.

You might be lucky enough to have a parent who lives close to the school who would provide a small yard area. The elderly couple across the street from the school might enjoy your children's garden in their yard. Or, there might be a vacant lot near the school that needs to be cleaned up and made productive once again.

Graphing, record keeping and measuring are just a few of many learning experiences your students would enjoy. Students could also create a map of the garden plot.

BOOKS TO ENJOY:

In Granny's Garden by Sarah Harrison, 1980, H. Holt and Company.

Three Stalks of Corn by Leo Politi, 1976, Macmillan.

GA1079

BULLETIN BOARD:

Background: blue paper

Border: empty seed packages—Use the seeds when you plant your class garden.

Make paper flibbers to resemble cornstalks. Directions may be found in the book *How to Make Flibbers*, etc., by Robert Lopshire. Attach your handy ears of corn to the flibber and mount to the bulletin board area.

An alternative cornstalk can be made by wrapping cardboard tubes from gift wrap with green crepe paper. Add green construction paper leaves.

ACTIVITY:

Have a study of the various vegetables that can be grown from seeds. Compare the size of the seed to the size of the plant.

Each day bring a different fresh vegetable to class. Many students have seen beets, zucchini, turnips, etc., only in the canned or frozen form. After a thorough examination, slice the fresh vegetable and let the students taste.

GA1079

Brave Banner

MATERIALS:

white paper cut in 5" x 7" pieces, wood dowel cut in 12" pieces, clay, crayons, scissors, glue

PROCEDURE:

Trace outline of the child's hand (fingers together) on white paper.

Draw star area and lines for the stripes.

Let children color and add stars.

Cut out flag shape and glue to the dowel rod.

Form small ball of clay into a base so the flagpole will stand.

A second smaller ball could be formed to create a ball for the top of the flagpole.

ACTIVITY ONE:

Play appropriate music and allow the students to march about the classroom carrying and waving the flags.

When the music stops, the students stand at attention and say the Pledge of Allegiance.

Paper hats with a patriotic flare could be made and worn while the students are marching.

Show pictures of other American flags so students will realize our flag has not always been the same.

ACTIVITY TWO:

Trace each child's hand a second time. Allow each child to create a family flag using any colors and design he wishes. One restriction might be that no red and white stripes or gold stars can be used.

GA1079

BULLETIN BOARD:

Background: white paper

Border: large yellow or gold foil stars each containing a child's name

Mount the flags about the bulletin board area. To do this remove the clay base. If your bulletin board is behind a table or shelf, you may want to set a few of the flags in front of the bulletin board.

Complete the bulletin board by:

a. adding pictures of historical sites.
b. adding pictures of faces of the wide variety of American people.
c. adding the flags or pictures of the flags of our fifty states.
d. adding pictures depicting activities that are a part of our lives because we are a free nation.
e. adding pictures of famous Americans.

ACTIVITY:

Build your activity based on how you decide to complete your bulletin board. Adding pictures of historical sites to complete the board would lead to a discussion of each place as well as a little map study to determine its location.

BOOKS TO ENJOY:

Did You Carry the Flag Today, Charley? by Rebecca Caudill, 1966, H. Holt and Company.

Flags by Brenda Thompson and Rosemary Giesen, 1977, Lerner Publications.

GA1079

Fireworks

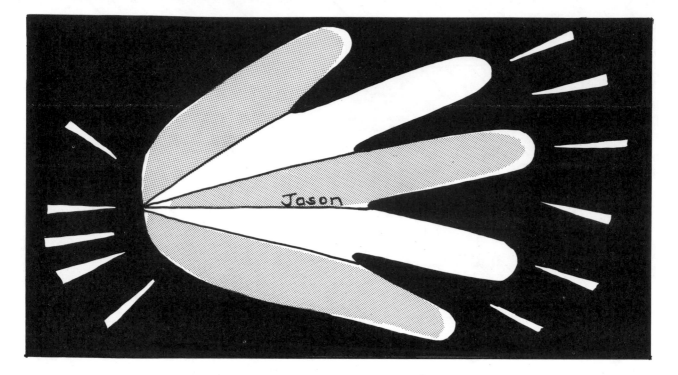

MATERIALS: red, green, blue, yellow and white paints; 9" x 12" piece of black construction paper

OPTIONAL: sequins and glue

PROCEDURE: Paint each child's palm and fingers an array of colors. Let the child choose one color per finger or two colors and alternate.

Press the painted hand firmly in the center of the black paper.

Allow time for drying.

With white or yellow paint, add streams of light around the handprint.

For a little extra sparkle, allow each child to glue a few sequins to the colorful explosion.

ACTIVITY: Have a birthday party celebration for our nation. Included in your party plans could be:

a. a birthday cake frosted red, white and blue.
b. a small flag for each child to carry and wave as he marches to patriotic music.
c. a large American flag hung on a wall of the party area.
d. a flag-raising ceremony complete with the Pledge of Allegiance to our flag.
e. listening to a story about our nation gaining its freedom.

BOOKS TO ENJOY: *Fourth of July Story* by Alice Dalgliesh, 1956, Scribners.

Fireworks, Picnics and Flags by James Giblin, Clarion Press.

GA1079

BULLETIN BOARD:

Background: black paper with sponge-painted stars

Border: silver or gold foil or white paper with silver or gold glitter

Attach the student-completed fireworks and poems about the bulletin board area.

Add bright paper graphics of sound words.

WRITING ACTIVITY:

No nighttime activity attracts as much attention as a fireworks display. Capture some of that "bursting in air" excitement with the following creative writing exercise. Brainstorm with your class some possibilities before students dictate poems to you.

Let's light up the sky with . . . . (given)

red	beams	sparkling	
yellow	streaks	soaring	(student
blue	bursts	popping	input)

What a birthday night . . . . (given)

GA1079

Liberty's Lady

Minh

MATERIALS:

5" x 7" pieces of light-green construction paper, crayons, markers, glue, 9" x 12" piece of white construction paper

PROCEDURE:

Trace each child's hand on the piece of green construction paper.

Add points to each fingertip as shown.

Using a black marker, outline facial features, crown and hair. Add neckline. Shade in with green crayon.

Cut out and glue onto the 9" x 12" sheet of white paper.

ACTIVITY ONE:

Help your students learn about this great statue and the immigrants that are greeted by her.

Read to the children *The Statue of Liberty* by Leonard Everett Fisher. Show pictures of the entire statue and tell about the recent renovation project and how all Americans contributed to the cost of the rejuvenation.

ACTIVITY TWO:

Remember the fun playing the traditional game Statues? After viewing pictures of The Statue of Liberty, let each child have a turn trying to pose like the gallant lady. Then play Statues. Children move about freely, with or without music. At unguarded moments shout, "Freeze." On hearing the word the children do just that. They become statues. If five children move at the same time and freeze and become statues, the remaining children can view and imagine what each frozen image might be.

BOOKS TO ENJOY:

Lady Liberty's Light by Barbara Birenbaum, 1986, Peartree.

Watch the Stars Come Out by Riki Levinson, 1985, Dutton.

GA1079

BULLETIN BOARD:

Background: gold foil paper

Border: green crepe paper fringed or scalloped and stapled into place or construction paper and tissue paper torches. Use the pattern below and staple crinkled tissue paper to the top before attaching to the bulletin board area.

Attach completed statues to the bulletin board area. Add faces of ethnic groups that represent the many faces of America to the bulletin board area.

EXTENSION:

Place a table or shelf in front of the bulletin board. Encourage students to bring a variety of statues from home to add to the display.

ACTIVITY:

It is time for a field trip. Visit a statue, monument, plaque or memorial in your community. Have a short lesson about its purpose and history. Visit a cemetery in your community and view the various ways people are remembered by their families, friends and the community.

TORCH PATTERN

Add various shades of crinkled tissue paper.

Squeeze cone into desired shape.

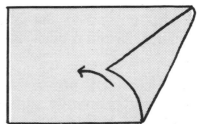

Roll green construction paper into cone shape.

GA1079

Summer Lily

MATERIALS:

12" x 18" sheet of blue paper; 5" x 7" sheet of white, yellow or orange paper; green paper for stem and leaves; scissors; glue; crayons

PROCECURE:

Trace each child's hand (all fingers extended). Cut out.

Fold thumb and baby finger inward so that the palm of the handprint forms a cone shape.

Glue fingers in place. Press flat.

Glue flower to 12" x 18" sheet of blue paper.

Cut stem from green paper or glue a green pipe cleaner to create the stem.

Shape leaves from green paper and add to stem area.

Draw in flower's center or create one from black pipe cleaner and glue in place.

ACTIVITY ONE:

In addition to those placed on the bulletin board, let each student make a second lily. These can be placed in a vase to create a bouquet for the reading table or teacher's desk.

Strengthen the stem by making it of green poster board or by wrapping a dowel rod or coat hanger with crepe paper or florist tape.

ACTIVITY TWO:

Take a summer flower-gathering stroll with your students. Find both culti-vated and wildflower varieties. Bring back to the classroom and press to preserve. Identify using a flower guide and create a scrapbook for the class to enjoy all year long.

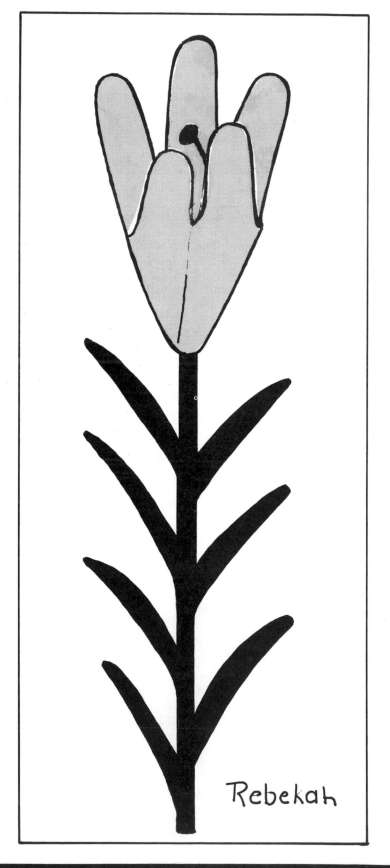

Rebekah

52

GA1079

BULLETIN BOARD ONE:

Background: yellow paper

Border: white scalloped crepe paper or construction paper—trim by gluing flower seeds to it.

Attach students' tall slender lilies about the bulletin board area. Add colorful pictures of other flowers.

BULLETIN BOARD TWO:

Background: white paper on which students have painted sky, ground and subsoil areas. A smiling sun, white billowy clouds, cool green grass, a butterfly, roots, a few rocks are just a few of the details that can be added.

Border: None is really needed, but one could be easily added by stapling 3″ strips of black construction paper around the bulletin board area.

*Instead of gluing completed lilies to the large sheets of blue construction paper, pin or tack them directly to the bulletin board. You will achieve a beautiful garden full of lilies by doing this. To further enhance the beauty of the garden, make the lilies a variety of shades of yellow and orange.

BOOKS TO ENJOY:

Summer Is Here! by Jane Moncure, 1975, Children's Press.

The Summer Night by Charlotte Zolotow, 1987, Harper.

GA1079

Fishing for Fun

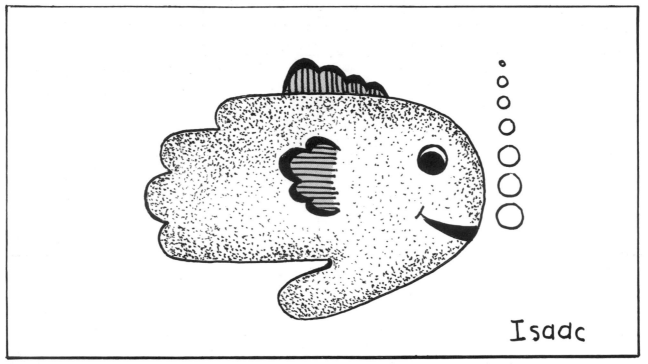

Isadc

MATERIALS: assorted colors of paper scraps, each 5" x 7"; fishnet material; 9" x 12" piece of blue paper; crayons; glue; scissors

PROCEDURE: Trace each child's hand, fingers together, thumb slightly extended.

Cut hand out and glue it (thumb toward bottom) to the 9" x 12" piece of paper.

Allow time to dry.

With crayons add fins and features. A child can do more than one fish. Each could be a different color. Face one fish the opposite direction. Have the child draw in some underwater plant life and cover the entire piece with the fishnet material for a very nautical look.

ACTIVITY ONE: Make several extra hand fish and attach paper clips to them. Put the fish in a small swimming pool (no water needed) and go fishing with a short pole made from a length of dowel rod with a magnet attached to the end of a string. Each paper fish could have a number printed on the back side to indicate the value. Your students will love "hooking the big ones."

ACTIVITY TWO: Teach observation skills by placing a couple of goldfish in a bowl in your classroom. Keep an observation chart. Allow each child the opportunity to observe the fish for five minutes. At the end of each observation period, allow the child to tell classmates what he saw.

Refine observation skills by asking questions similar to the following:
a. Did both fish swim in the same direction?
b. Did you see bubbles? When? Where?
c. Did the fish eat while you observed?
d. Did either of the fish go to the surface of the water?
e. What parts of the fish did you see move?

GA1079

BULLETIN BOARD:

Background: blue paper sponge painted to resemble water

Border: seashells, either paper ones or real ones

A final touch of an old fishnet covering the entire bulletin board area would be nice but not necessary.

ALTERNATE:

Instead of mounting the fish made from the students' hands to sheets of blue paper, pin them about the bulletin board area. Students can use white paint to make bubbles and green paint to add plant life.

ACTIVITY:

Collect several pairs of swim fins, goggles, masks and snorkle tubes. Play appropriate music and allow the students to move about the room pretending they are swimmers watching fish.

Change the music. Collect the snorkeling equipment and have the students pretend to be fish who are watching humans swim and snorkle.

BOOKS TO ENJOY:

Fish Is Fish by Leo Lionni, 1970, Pantheon.

Swimmy by Leo Lionni, 1963, Pantheon.

GA1079

Crazy Eights

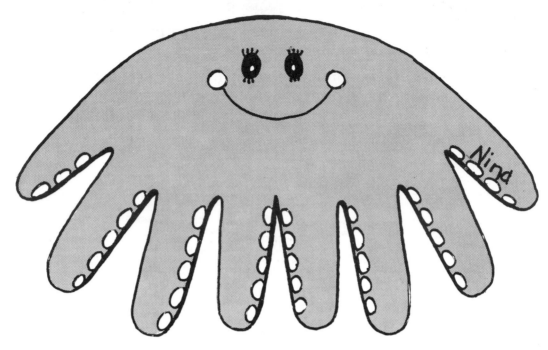

MATERIALS: 5″ x 7″ pieces of light-blue construction paper, white poster board cut into 6″ x 9″ pieces, blue and white paint, small paper cups (to hold paint), Q-tips, scissors, glue, crayons

PROCEDURE: Paint both hands of each student blue; omit thumbs.

Press onto light-blue paper and let dry.

Turn so fingers are pointed down and use crayons to create a face.

Dip Q-tip in white paint and daub tentacles on inside as shown in the example. Allow time for drying and cut out.

Glue the octopus to the center of the 6″ x 9″ piece of white poster board and add symbols to create a playing card for the card game Crazy Eights.

ACTIVITY: Practice math facts. Make a large octopus with detachable arms. On the arms (you will need more than eight) print numerals 0-20 as well as a plus, a minus and an equal sign. Let the students practice creating problems that equal the answer eight.

Arms can be attached to the octopus in sequential order. Some tentacles could have the word (seven) for the numeral printed on them.

 GA1079

BULLETIN BOARD:

Background: black and white striped paper or paint black strips on white paper

Border: red construction paper as shown or glue a deck of playing cards to the background paper

Arrange octopus playing cards in "hands" for a card game effect.

Add student writing about the board area. The student writing could be printed on card game scorecards.

WRITING ACTIVITY:

Having eight arms might have its advantages. Brainstorm with your students some possibilities. Make a list on a chart as ideas are stated. Let each child select ideas to incorporate into the writing form illustrated below.

I wish I had eight arms ....(given)

to hug everyone in my family all at once
to clean up my room in a flash   } (student input)
to do all my homework with more time to play

Being a "handy" person would be GREAT! ....(given)

BOOKS TO ENJOY:

Herman the Helper Cleans Up by Robert Kraus, 1981, Windmill Books.

Otto Is Different by Franz Brandenberg, 1985, Greenwillow.

GA1079

Sunshine, You're Mine

Matt

MATERIALS: 3" or 4" yellow circles, 9" x 12" sheet of orange paper, scissors, glue, crayons, orange paint

PROCEDURE: Paint each child's hand orange.

With a pencil put a dot in the center of the orange paper and make the handprints around it in a clockwise fashion. Let dry.

Use a crayon to make a face on the yellow circle.

Glue the circle in the center of the handprints.

Cut out and display.

ACTIVITY: Make and wear paper sunglasses. Use colored cellophane as lenses.

Take the children outside and play shadow tag.

BOOKS TO ENJOY: *Sun Up, Sun Down* by Gail Gibbons, 1983, Harcourt.

Wake Up, Sun by David Harrison, 1986, Random House.

GA1079

BULLETIN BOARD:

Background: white paper

Border: display the paper sunglasses the children made

Use straight pins to mount the student-made suns. This will create a three-dimensional effect. Fluffy blue clouds could be glued or taped to the board area behind the sun. Add homonym pair cards to the board. Place a pocket on the bottom of the board. In it place a second set of the homonym cards for the students to work.

ACTIVITY:

Sun has a homonym—*son.* Select an appropriate number of homonym pairs for your students to study. Each pair should be printed on construction paper as shown below. Students can practice matching the homonyms or playing a concentration game.

To play Concentration turn all cards face down on a flat surface. Students in turn select two cards. If the two words chosen are homonyms, the student keeps the cards and takes another turn. If they are not, the word cards are returned to their face-down position. Part of the fun is remembering the position of exposed words. Part of the fun is learning the homonym pairs.

too/two	one/won	see/sea	be/bee
in/inn	no/know	you/ewe	tee/tea
four/fore	tin/ten	him/hem	ate/eight
I/eye	pair/pear	cent/sent	right/write

GA1079

Clowning Around

Justin

Kelly

MATERIALS: 5" x 7" piece of white paper, various colors of yarn scraps, tiny red pom-poms (could be any color), material scraps, crayons, paint, scissors, glue

PROCEDURE: Paint just the fingers and thumb of the child.

Color of paint can vary but will set the color coordination for the entire project.

Press firmly to make print on the piece of white paper.

Draw a clown face inside the print. The face could be drawn on a pink construction paper circle. If so, then glue the circle just above the fingerprint.

Use a pom-pom for a nose.

Glue various colors of yarn scraps to create shocks of hair.

Cut a hat pattern from an index card or manila folder and use to create hats from the scraps of material. Glue in place.

A second pom-pom can be glued to the top of the hat.

If desired, cut out and glue the clown head to a large sheet of white paper. The children can then draw and color the body.

ACTIVITY: Make a larger clown from your handprint. Outline the body and print body parts in appropriate places.

Body parts could be printed on small cards and the children could practice putting them in the correct places.

BULLETIN BOARD: Background: blue paper on which you have painted a bright red and white striped circus tent

Place completed faces or clowns about the bulletin board area. Add some student-created writing. Use the sample below.

CREATIVE WRITING: Capture some of your "clowning around" fun by brainstorming things that happen when you are a clown.

We are clowning around today: . . . . (given)

making faces,
doing magic tricks,   (student
teaching dogs to jump through hoops   input)
juggling balls and wearing polka-dots.

Isn't it fun! . . . . (given)

BOOKS TO ENJOY: *The Clown of God* by Tomie de Paola, Scholastic.

The Clown-Arounds by Joanna Cole, 1981, Parents.

GA1079

Happy Birthday

MATERIALS:

5" x 7" piece of white paper, crayons, glue, scissors, several colors of paint

PROCEDURE:

Paint the fingers and thumb of a child's hand one color and the palm of the child's hand another color.

Press painted hand on white paper to make a print. Allow time for drying.

With yellow crayon draw candle glows.

Use other colors of crayons to decorate the cake. Use a black crayon to outline a plate.

If desired, mount the entire creation on a 6" x 8" piece of colored construction paper.

ACTIVITY:

Graph birthday information for your class. Chart how many birthdays occur each month of the year.

If you have students of various ages, you may also wish to chart the ages.

On a calendar let each child print his name in the appropriate date.

You can also graph what kind of cake each child likes. You may wish to make a note of each child's preference.

Ask each child what color balloon he would like for his birthday. Graph these findings. Also record the information. On the child's birthday make a large paper balloon. Use yarn for string. Print *Happy Birthday*, _____ on the balloon and attach to the classroom door on the appropriate day.

Look at other simple graphs found in magazines, books and newspapers. Discuss how graphs can be used and why they are good to use.

GA1079

BULLETIN BOARD: Background: birthday wrapping paper

Border: possibilities include party favors, old birthday cards, ribbon and bows

Divide the bulletin board area into twelve sections, one for each month. Label the months. Have each child place his "handmade" birthday cake in the proper section.

Print the date of the child's birthday on the plate that holds his cake.

This display could be used all year.

Don't forget to display the various graphs that were created from the birthday information.

BOOKS TO ENJOY: *Birthday Party* by Ruth Krauss, 1957, Harper Jr. Books.

Happy Birthday! by Gail Gibbons, 1986, Holiday.

REFERENCE BOOK: *Parties for Home and School* by Lamb and Bellows, 1985, Good Apple, Inc.

ANOTHER IDEA: On his special day let the child choose a book he would like the teacher to read to the class. The birthday child can introduce the listening session and tell his peers the name of the book he has chosen and why he chose the book.

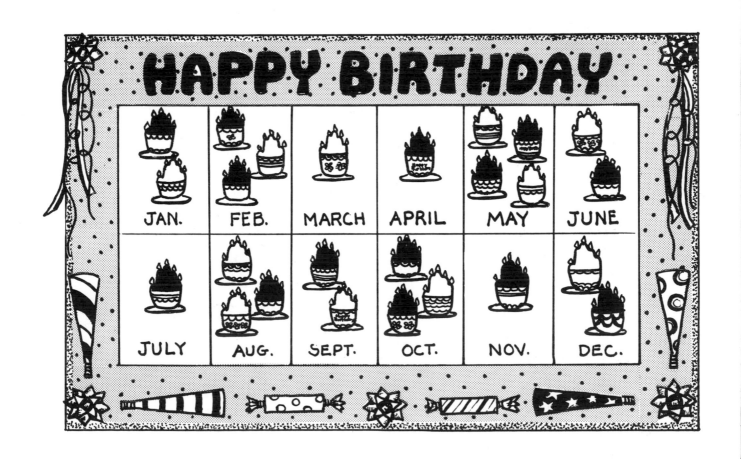

GA1079

Leaf Dancer

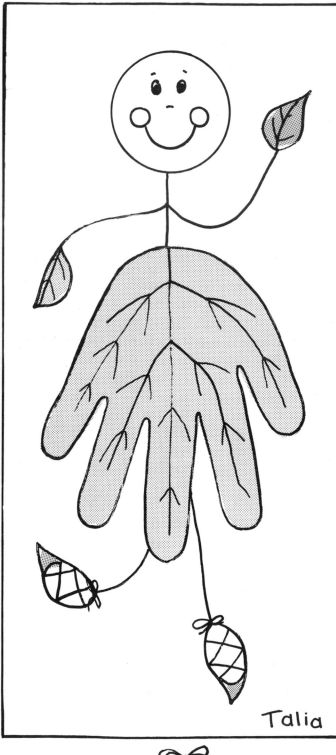

Talia

MATERIALS:
9" x 12" piece of drawing paper, crayons, black marker

PROCEDURE:
Use a black marker to outline each child's hand. Fingers should be pointing down.

*Before having the children complete their handprints, show some pictures or a film of ballet dancers. The results of the project will be more varied when the children are better acquainted with the possible positions a "leaf dancer" could create.

The child then uses the crayons to create a leaf dancer using the outlined handprint as a costume.

ACTIVITY:
Let the leaf dancers inspire some creative movement in your classroom.

Play some appropriate music and encourage your children to move about as a leaf would when:
a. being blown by a gentle breeze.
b. falling to the ground on a crisp autumn afternoon.
c. opening to enjoy the warmth of a spring sun.
d. enduring a sudden summer thunderstorm.
e. showing its bright fall colors.
f. bracing for an unexpected early frost and snowfall.

BOOKS TO ENJOY:
Harriet's Recital by Nancy Carlson, 1985, Penguin Books, Inc.

Angelina Ballerina by Katherine Holabird, 1983, Crown.

GA1079

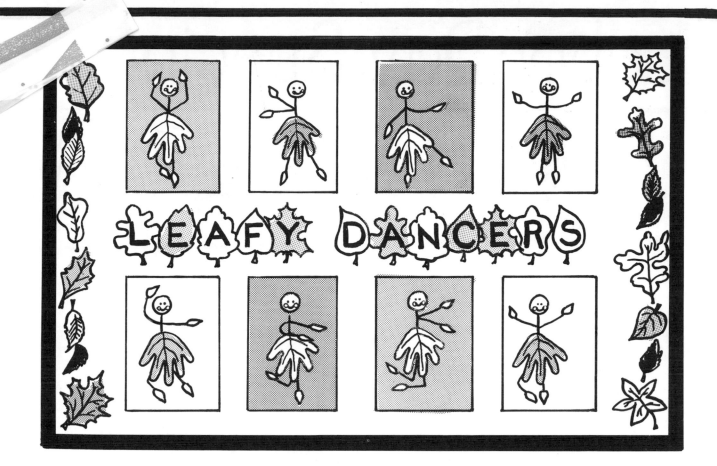

BULLETIN BOARD:

Background: brown wrapping paper

Border: real leaves, take your class on a hike and collect a colorful variety

Lettering: With a black marker, print appropriate letters on construction paper leaf shapes of various fall colors.

You may wish to mount each student creation on a sheet of red, yellow, brown or orange construction paper.

Attach leaf dancers in straight rows to the bulletin board area to resemble a dancing troupe.

ACTIVITY:

Here is a chance for your students to become leaf choreographers. Have each child dictate the steps his leaf dancer will take. Let the example below serve as a model from which to create the student writing.

Little leaf . . . . given line
Spin around . . . . verb phrase
Turn around . . . . verb phrase
Jump up high . . . . verb phrase
Touch the sky . . . . verb phrase
Take a bow . . . . verb phrase
Do a dance for fall . . . . given line

GA1079

Labor Day Special

MATERIALS: 10" circle of white paper, pencil, crayons

PROCEDURE: Place hand with fingers closed, thumb slightly extended on the center of the circle of paper.

Using the pencil, trace the outline of the hand lightly.

Turn upside down and fashion each laborer using the thumb area for the nose and the fingers for the chin.

Add hats to represent different professions.

Results will be much better if younger children are shown several examples.

ACTIVITY: To aid your students in understanding the celebration of Labor Day, have them join in creating new verses for the song below. It can be sung to the tune of "The Farmer in the Dell."

> The teacher uses her brain.
> The teacher uses her brain.
> This is the way she works each day.
> The teacher uses her brain.

Other verses: The farmer drives his tractor.
> The carpenter uses his saw.
> The waiter serves the food.
> The model looks so pretty.
> The banker counts the coins.

Place all your handy worker pictures in a class book and sing a new verse as you flip each page.

GA1079

Let's Work

BULLETIN BOARD:

Background: any color of paper

Border: paper money

Mount the white circle portraits on 9" x 12" sheets of construction paper that coordinate with the color of the background paper.

Add student writing to bottom of portrait.

Pictures of workers from magazines can also be placed about the bulletin board area.

WRITING ACTIVITY:

Have each student brainstorm activities that his worker might do during a typical work day. Use the student input to create a writing similar to the example below.

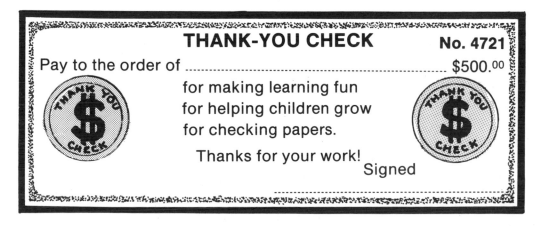

THANK-YOU CHECK   **No. 4721**

Pay to the order of $500.⁰⁰

for making learning fun
for helping children grow
for checking papers.

Thanks for your work!

Signed

BOOKS TO ENJOY:

When We Grow Up by Anne Rockwell, 1981, Dutton.

Richard Scarry's Busiest People Ever by Richard Scarry, 1976, Random House.

Who Does What by Eric Hill, 1982, Price, Stern.

    GA1079

Autumn Handful

MATERIALS:

9" x 12" drawing paper, 9" x 12" piece of brown paper, small sponge, paint (red, yellow, orange), glue, pencil, scissors

PROCEDURE:

Place arm and hand on sheet of paper.

Trace lightly, using the pencil and cut out tracing.

Glue cutout pattern to the sheet of drawing paper.

Paint on autumn leaves with the sponges.

DISPLAY:

Instead of creating a bulletin board, place trees along the chalkboard in a colorful row.

ACTIVITY:

Take an autumn stroll with your class. Have the children note the structure of fall trees and the variety of color in their leaves.

This is a good time to spot some evergreen trees. Ask students why they stay green. Provide input to aid their understanding.

Collect some of the most colorful leaves and take them back to the classroom for decorating.

Use black paint or a black marker to draw faces on some leaves.

BOOKS TO ENJOY:

Ring of Earth: *A Child's Book of Seasons* by Jane Yolen, 1986, Harcourt.

The Seasons of Arnold's Apple Tree by Gail Gibbons, 1984, Harcourt.

Four Stories for Four Seasons by Tomie de Paola, 1977, Treehouse.

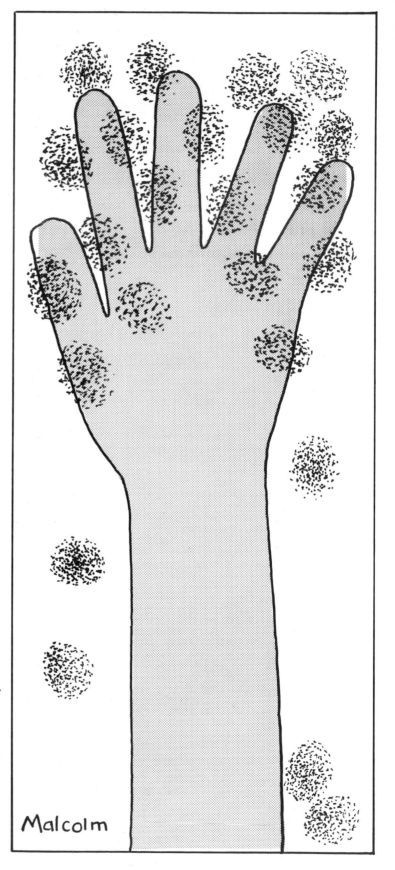

Malcolm

GA1079

Autumn Handfuls

BULLETIN BOARD:

Background: light brown craft or wrapping paper

Border: leaves that have been gathered while on a nature hike

Mount painted, cutout trees to bulletin board area in clusters.

Print names of trees (maple, elm, oak) on index cards. Place about the bulletin board area. These cards could be attached to samples of leaves from various trees in your area.

ACTIVITY ONE:

Fall also allows trees to show other signs of its identity—bark, nuts, twigs, etc.

On a nature hike collect appropriate items. Place these on display near the bulletin board area.

ACTIVITY TWO:

Scramble the names of common trees. Print the scrambled name on one card. On a second card print the name of the tree. Let students take turns matching cards. Older students may not need the matching cards but could print correct names on a numbered answer sheet.

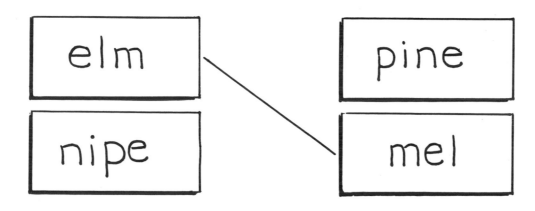

Butterfly Flutter By

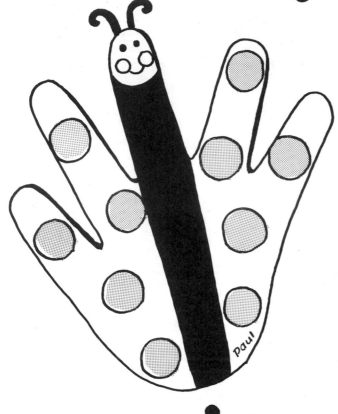

MATERIALS:

paint, crayons, scissors, sheets of white paper

PROCEDURE:

Paint palm and fingers of the child's hand according to the diagram below.

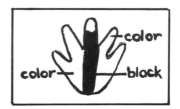

Press hand onto white paper to make the butterfly print. Let dry.

Add face and markings and antennae.

Cut out butterfly and hang suspended from the classroom ceiling. You could stretch a wire across the corner of the classroom. Use clear fishing line to hang the butterflies.

ACTIVITY:

Assign homework before doing this art activity. Send each child on a search-and-find mission to capture a butterfly or a picture from a magazine. Study the pictures and the examples for inspiration when painting the hand versions.

Remember to set the live butterflies free after studying them.

BOOKS TO ENJOY:

Where Does the Butterfly Go When It Rains? by May Garelick, 1970, Scholastic.

Look-a-Butterfly by David Cutts, 1982, Troll Associates.

Hi Butterfly by Taro Gomi, 1985, Morrow Jr. Books.

GA1079

BULLETIN BOARD:

Background: a plain color of paper, maybe light blue or yellow

Border: flowers made from construction paper

Attach brightly colored yarn to butterflies and place them about the bulletin board area. This will allow them to flutter freely.

Tape the other end of the yarn to the card or paper containing the writing activity.

ALTERNATE:

Make large flowers including stem and leaves from construction paper.

Attach a butterfly to each and place about the classroom.

ACTIVITY:

Let each student create a written dance for his butterfly. Follow the format presented below.

Little butterfly ....flutter by ....(given)
dance a ballet ....(action)
in my autumn garden.......................................(place)
today...(time)

The last three lines of the poem are student input. Older students could have additional phrases before the last line.

Mr. Wise Guy

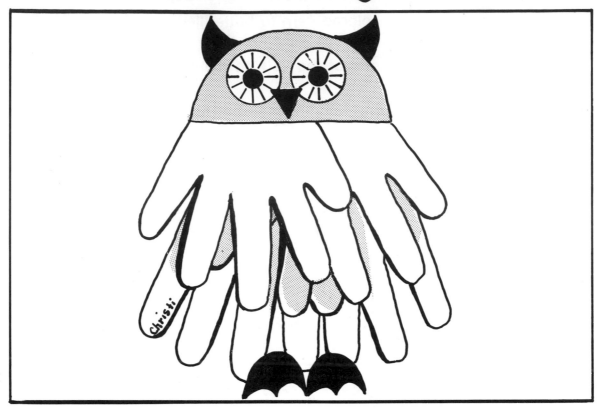

MATERIALS: brown, orange, yellow construction paper; crayons; glue; scissors

PROCEDURE: Trace the child's hand four times on yellow and orange paper. Cut out all four patterns.

Make the owl's head from a semicircle of brown paper.

Add eyes and a beak with the crayons.

Glue hands together as shown.

Glue head on top of hands.

Curl edges of fingers forward for a feathered look.

ACTIVITY: Play an autumn game of owl charades. One child is chosen to be the owl. He must act out what he sees from his perch in the forest. The other children guess until one correctly determines what Mr. Wise Eyes is viewing. The correct guesser gets to be the next Mr. Wise Guy.

This is an excellent tool for teaching your children about the forest environment. Following are some excellent books to help you do this.

BOOKS TO ENJOY: *The Owl Book* by Laura Storms, 1983, Lerner Publications.

Good-Night Owl by Pat Hutchins, 1972, Macmillan.

Owliver by Robert Kraus, 1974, Windmill Books.

GA1079

BULLETIN BOARD: Background: a golden yellow or night shade of grey or blue

Border: scalloped and of a contrasting color

From black or brown paper, cut a large tree. Place the completed Mr. Wise Guys on the branches.

Poems can be printed on large paper leaves and placed near the owls.

You may wish to add a large autumn moon in the background.

ACTIVITY: Make three sets of cards. On one set paste pictures of animals. On the second set print the name of the animal. On the third set print the word for the sound the animal makes.

Students can group cards in correct groups.

cow	picture	moo
pig	picture	oink
sheep	picture	baa
dog	picture	bow-wow

Shuffle the picture cards. Students take turns choosing a card and making the appropriate sound. Fellow students guess the animal.

GA1079

Sail on, Columbus

MATERIALS: 9" x 12" piece of blue paper, 5" x 7" piece of brown paper, scraps of white paper, crayon, scissors, glue, blue paint

PROCEDURE: Trace the child's hand with thumb and baby finger extended. The three middle fingers should be pointed straight and slightly spread. This should be done on a piece of brown paper. Cut out.

With a black crayon, section off the palm from the thumb to the baby finger as shown in the example.

Color after making three or four portholes with the black crayon.

Cut out and glue fluffy white sails to the three middle fingers. Designs may be added to any or all of the sails.

Cut out and glue entire ship to sheet of blue paper.

Paint the ocean blue.

Add flag if desired.

ACTIVITY: Read a story about the voyage of Christopher Columbus. Do your creative pretending to re-create his voyage.

Put all the desks or tables together in the center of the classroom to form a make-believe ship and have everyone hop on board.

Sing sailing songs and discuss what the voyage to the New World might have been like.

BOOKS TO ENJOY: A Book About Christopher Columbus by Ruth Gross, 1975, Scholastic.

I, Christopher Columbus by Lisl Weil, 1983, Macmillan.

Christopher Columbus, Who Sailed On by Dorothy Richards, 1978, Child's World.

GA1079

BULLETIN BOARD:

Background: light blue or white paper

Border: dark-blue paper cut in an ocean wave shape or 5″ round circles of old maps that have been mounted on slightly larger circles of brown paper

Mount finished ships in groups of three.

ACTIVITY:

Display a variety of maps. Included could be an atlas, an encyclopedia, a road map, etc. Allow students time to look at the maps and discuss what they see. Point out a few basic concepts. For example, the top of a map is always north.

On a large sheet of white paper, create a map of the classroom. Start with just the outline (perimeter). Indicate where the door is and where the windows are located. Have students suggest other things to show on the map. As they are mentioned, cut small pieces of construction paper and glue in appropriate places. Be sure to indicate each student's seat by printing his initials. Without getting too technical, continue until interest wanes.

A few days later give each child the opportunity to contribute to a map of the playground or the block on which the school is located.

GA1079

Let's Go Batty

Marisa

MATERIALS: 9" x 12" piece of black construction paper folded in half, crayons, scissors, string or clear plastic fishing line

PROCEDURE: Place hand thumb up and fingers spread on the fold. See illustration above.

Trace lightly and cut out.

Open and add your bat's features with crayons or bits of construction paper glued on in the proper places.

From the scraps of black paper cut out some feet and attach with a drop of glue.

Create facial features on both sides of the bat. Use tape to attach a length of the fishing line and hang about the classroom at various levels for some spooky fun.

ACTIVITY: Play a singing Halloween game to the tune of "Skip to My Lou." Have your children form a circle and choose five students to enter the center as bats.

Sing three verses to complete each game.

Verse 1: Little black bats turn around. (3 times)
Halloween is coming.

Verse 2: Little black bats fly around. (3 times)
Halloween is coming.

Verse 3: Little black bats bite someone. (3 times)
Halloween is coming.

Instead of biting, children should tap those chosen to be the next set of bats.

GA1079

BULLETIN BOARD:

Background: grey paper—cut cone-shaped stalagtites of shades of brown and black, overlap and spread across the top of the grey background

In this spooky cave students will hang their bats.

No border is needed.

Attach bats at the end of the stalagtites. Leave wings (fingers) free. You may wish to hang some of the bats with fishing line in front of the bulletin board area.

On additional pieces of brown and black construction paper shaped like rocks, glue student writing.

WRITING ACTIVITY:

Let the students go "batty" brainstorming all *b* words for these silly bat stories. Make sure you think of nouns, verbs, adjectives and adverbs. Poems can be presented in free form.

Black bats bite.
Black bats bite boys.
Bob, Bill, Ben, Brian,
Brett, Barry, Brad
Boooooo! Boooooo!

Big black bats
Bite
Bite
Bite
bawling babies
bad boys and
buzzing bees.

BOOKS TO ENJOY:

Little Bat's Secret by Kathy Darling, 1974, Garrard.

Spooky and the Wizard's Bats by Natalie Carlson, 1986, Lothrop.

Lavinia Bat by Russell Hoban, 1984, H. Holt and Company.

GA1079

Splatter Ghostie

Jonathan

MATERIALS:
9" x 12" piece of white paper, black paint, spray bottle, water, stiff paperlike manila folders, scissors, scraps of black paper

PROCEDURE:
Trace outline of child's hand on stiff paper. Cut out and place securely on white paper.

Spray entire surface with black paint diluted with water.

Remove hand shape.

Glue circles of black paper to make eyes and nose.

ACTIVITY: Play a game of Boo-Who with your students. Ask the children to form a circle. While they are moving about, secretly select one child to leave the room to become the ghost. Provide the ghost with a white sheet costume. When the circle is complete, the ghost returns and the children must guess who the "boo" is. Keep playing with different ghosts and a newly formed circle each time.

If playing outside, students can close their eyes while the "boo" is being selected.

BOOKS TO ENJOY: *Ghost's Hour, Spook's Hour* by Eve Bunting, 1987, Clarion.

Boo! Who? by Colin and Jacqui Hawkins, 1983, H. Holt and Company.

Amanda and the Giggling Ghost by Steven Kroll, 1980, Holiday.

BULLETIN BOARD: Background: sponge-paint black paper with white paint

Border: none needed

Attach the ghost pictures about the bulletin board area. Add completed student writing for a hauntingly good display.

WRITING ACTIVITY: Ghosts are busy fellows on Halloween. Capture some of their many activities in a student-created poem. The following model will guide you.

GHOSTIES!

verbs { howl . . . at the moon
scream . . . in the dark
fly . . . near the stars
flutter . . by my window
tiptoe . . . along the street
and say "Boo" on Halloween! } prepositional phrases

ACTIVITY: The word *ghost* has a silent letter. Bet a spook of some kind just slipped it in to trick human beings.

Make a list of simple words, each of which has a silent letter. Print each word on a card. Hold the card up for students to see and determine which letter is the tricky silent letter.

After discovering the silent letters, "treat" your Halloween detectives to a bat or ghost-shaped cookie.

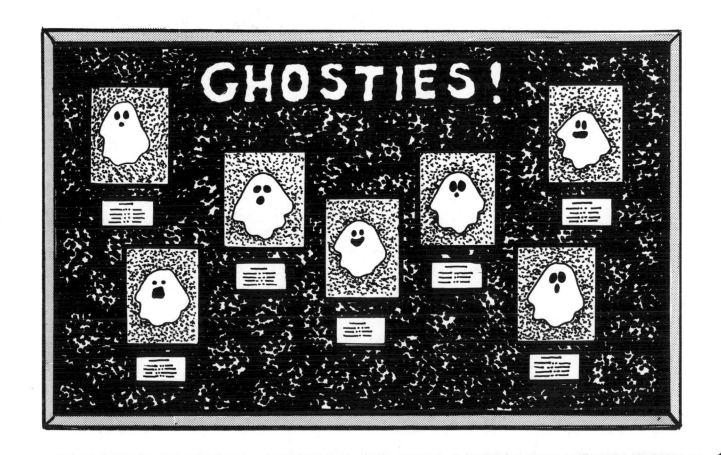

GA1079

Hands for Peace

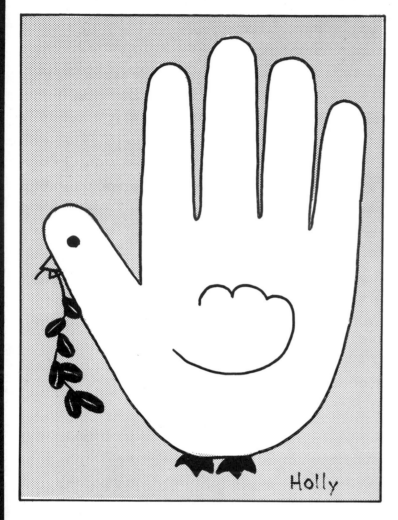

Holly

MATERIALS:
5" x 7" piece of light-blue construction paper, white paint and crayons

PROCEDURE:
Paint each child's palm and fingers with white paint.

Holding hand with fingers together and thumb extended, press hard to make print.

Let dry. Add wing, feet, eye and beak with crayons.

Outline with black crayon or marker.

Add sprig of leaves with crayon or find a tiny piece of leaf greenery at a craft store. Cut to appropriate sized pieces. Cut beak with a single-edged razor blade. Attach the sprig of silk greenery by placing it under beak and taping it in place from the back side.

ACTIVITY:
To celebrate Veterans' Day, introduce your students to some modern day "peacemakers." Consult a *World Almanac* for a listing of recent Nobel Prize winners. Then research a little.

Choose a person from a country other than America to reinforce the idea that many nations have veterans. They may celebrate the occasion on a different date, but they do honor those who served to bring peace to the world.

*This activity could be used to celebrate United Nations Day as well as Veterans' Day.

BOOKS TO ENJOY:
The Prince and the Lute by Kurt Baumann, 1986, H. Holt and Company.

The Bird with the Word Talks About Peace by Claudia Rees, 1987, Harrison House.

GA1079

BULLETIN BOARD:

Background: On white paper, project a map of the world and draw the outline of the continents.

Border: strips of paper of various colors cut about 2½" wide. On each use a marker to print the name of a nation of the world.

Attach peace birds in various locations to indicate the nation of a famous "peacemaker."

On cards print the name of the leader.

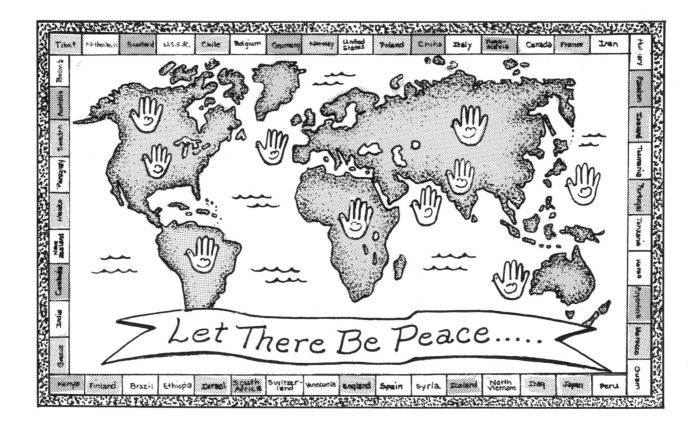

Let There Be Peace.....

ACTIVITY:

Have short teacher-led class discussions. Topics to briefly explore could include:

a. What is the opposite of peace?
b. What happens to cause a war?
c. Why is peace better than war?
d. What can each of us do to help the world be peaceful?
e. Compare and contrast war to a fight with a brother or sister or a classmate.

GA1079

Indian Assistance

MATERIALS:

9″ x 12″ white drawing paper, 9″ x 12″ brown construction paper, crayons, glue, scissors

PROCEDURE:

Trace child's hand on the white drawing paper. Fingers and thumb should be pointed up and slightly extended.

Draw lines to create a headband where the fingers meet the palm.

Decorate the headband and create feathers from the fingers.

Round the palm to create a chin and jawline. Add hair.

Add facial features.

Use the patterns provided to create the body.

Use the crayons to add detail to the clothing and body.

Cut out and mount to the brown paper.

If you desire, use the scissors to fringe the brown on all four sides.

ACTIVITY:

Let these student-made Native Americans help your class learn about Thanksgiving and the first Americans.

Explain that the term *Indian* refers to a race of people just as the terms *Black, Hispanic, Asian* and *Caucasian* do.

Various Indian tribes like Sioux, Hopi, Crow, etc., are people of the race much the same as French, German, English and Canadian. Tell about various groups of Caucasians.

Use information found in reference books to help you present your information about the first Americans.

82

GA1079

BOOKS TO ENJOY:

Squanto and the First Thanksgiving by Joyce K. Kessel, 1983, Carolrhoda Books.

The Story of the Pilgrims and Their Indian Friends by Eunice Cauper, 1984, Branden Publishing Co.

BULLETIN BOARD:

Background: yellow paper

Border: bright colors of paper feathers

Place student-made Native Americans about the bulletin board area.

Add pictures of Indians and how they live today as well as pictures of their ancestors who lived in America long before we were born.

On cards print the names of various Indian tribes.

GA1079

Grapeful Harvest

MATERIALS:

5" x 7" pieces of white drawing paper, black marker, purple and green crayons, multicolored pieces of paper, glue, scissors, stapler

PROCEDURE:

Trace each child's hand (fingers and thumb together) on a sheet of white drawing paper.

At the top of the palm add a stem and grape leaves.

With the black marker, outline the traced hand, leaves and stem and draw circles to completely cover the hand area.

Use the crayons to color the grapes and leaves.

Cut out and mount on a colored sheet of paper and place on the bulletin board.

ALTERNATE:

Do not mount the bunches of grapes onto the paper. Use them with leaves (pattern follows) to create a border for your bulletin board.

BOOKS TO ENJOY:

Fried Feathers for Thanksgiving by James Stevenson, 1986, Greenwillow Press.

It's Thanksgiving! by Jack Prelutsky, 1987, Scholastic.

Thanksgiving at the Tappleton's by Eileen Spinelli, 1984, Harper Jr.

ACTIVITY:

Make a paper cornucopia filled with your handy grapes and various other fruits and vegetables of the autumn harvest season.

Cut a large semicircle from brown paper and staple it into a cone shape to make a horn of plenty.

Use a brown marker or crayon to create a woven pattern.

Draw and cut out other fruits from appropriate colors of paper to create the various fruits and vegetables.

Use this bountiful display as the center of your bulletin board display.

84

GA1079

BULLETIN BOARD: Background: yellow, orange or green paper

Border: student-made clusters of grapes

Place large cornucopia in center. About this focal point place student writing.

ALTERNATE: Let each student choose which fruits and vegetables he would like in his cornucopia. Each child can add his cluster of grapes.

Place completed student projects about the bulletin board area. Also place cards about the bulletin board. On each card should be printed the name of a fruit or vegetable.

WRITING ACTIVITY: Celebrate this fruitful holiday by writing a verse about this bountiful time of year. Brainstorm a list of fruits and vegetables and words to describe them. From this list students will create a verse modeled from the following example.

```
My cornucopia overflows with .............................(given)
juicy, purple, grapes.....................(adjective, adjective, noun)
crunchy, brown walnuts ................(adjective, adjective, noun)
sweet golden corn.......................(adjective, adjective, noun)
delicious red apples ....................(adjective, adjective, noun)
What a tummy, yummy holiday..............................(given)
```

A Grapeful Harvest

GA1079

FRUIT AND VEGETABLE PATTERNS

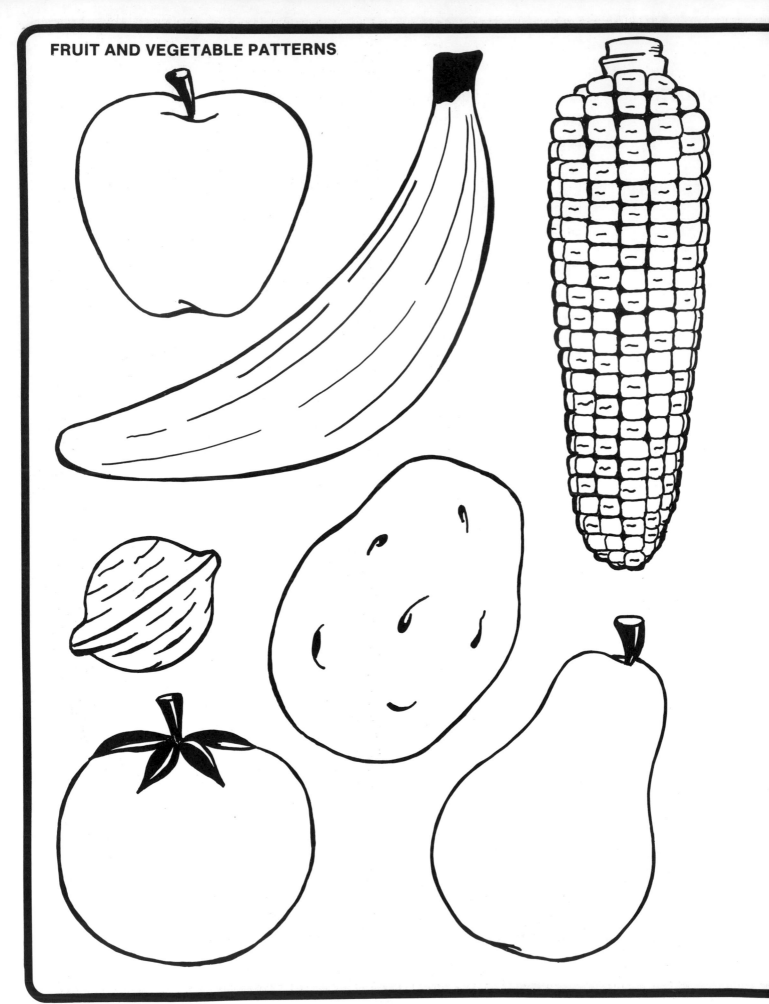

86

GA1079

**CORNUCOPIA
PATTERN**

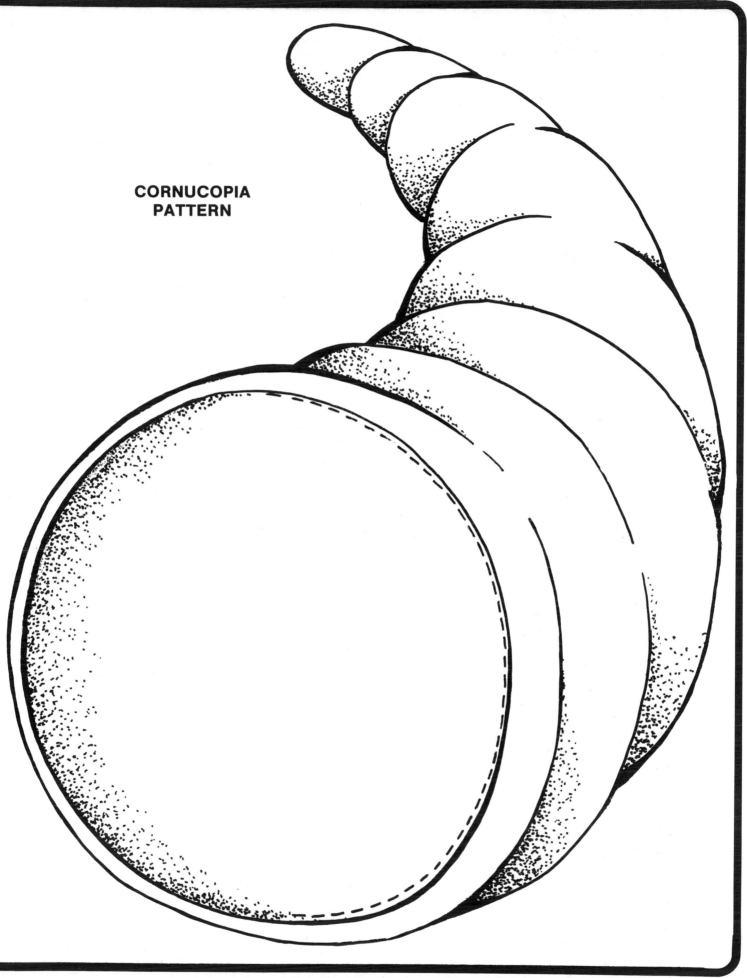

GA1079

Pilgrim Fathers !
Pilgrim Mothers !

Steven

MATERIALS: white paper cut in 10″ circles, black paper, yellow paper, glue, crayons

PROCEDURE: Trace each child's hand on black paper (thumb and littlest finger extended). The three middle fingers should be pointed straight and held tightly together. Use a rubber band to help hold the three middle fingers together while tracing.

Cut trimming off palm section.

Make a band from yellow paper and glue on the hat.

Glue pilgrim hat onto the white circle of paper and draw pilgrim face and collar.

Body patterns for pilgrims follow.

AUTHOR'S NOTE: I must admit I tried and tried but could not create the pilgrim lady from a handprint. But the pattern for the pilgrim lady is included.

BOOKS TO ENJOY: *The Pilgrims of Plimoth* by Marcia Sewall, 1986, Atheneum Children's Books.

The Coming of the Pilgrims by E. Brooks Smith and Robert Meredith, 1976, Little, Brown and Company.

GA1079

BULLETIN BOARD:

Background: black paper

Border: ruffled blue crepe paper

Attach pilgrims about the bulletin board area in neat rows. This should resemble a gallery at a museum.

Beneath each portrait place the appropriate student writing.

WRITING ACTIVITY:

Honor the original Pilgrim Fathers and Pilgrim Mothers by doing some investigation into their lives. The *World Book Encyclopedia* has a listing of all the passengers on the *Mayflower*. You can use part history and part fantasy to achieve your writing success. Use original names, add adjectives for description and a statement about each Pilgrim. The following models illustrate one means of presentation.

Edward Winslow tall and strong He built the first home in Plymouth. 1620	Governor John Carver smart and courageous He wrote laws for the Pilgrims. 1620

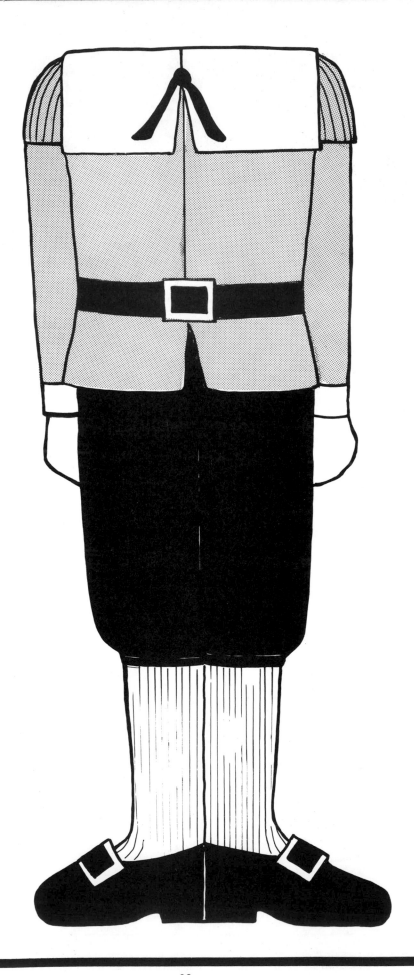

GA1079

91

Menorah Magic

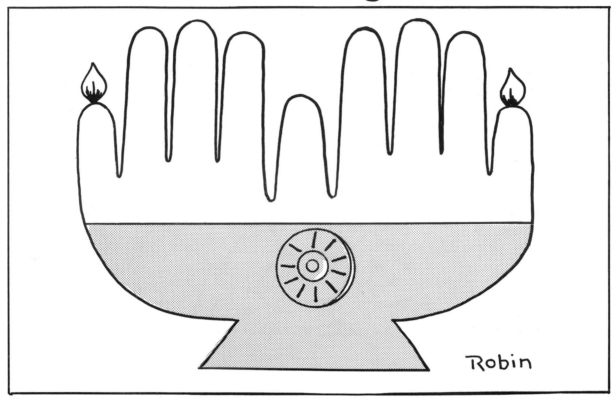

Robin

MATERIALS: sheet of white drawing paper, crayons, glue, scissors, yellow paper or gold foil

PROCEDURE: Fold a sheet of white paper in half and trace the child's hand.

Cut out both hands and glue them together at the thumbs. Trim carefully so the thumbs seem to be just one.

From the yellow paper or gold foil paper, cut out a menorah base.

Glue the base to the hands covering part of the palms.

Glue the completed menorah to another large sheet of paper and draw the candle glows and color.

BOOKS TO ENJOY: *The Eight Nights: A Chanukah Counting Book* by Jane Bearman, 1979, UAHC.

My First Hanukkah Book by Aileen Fisher, 1985, Children's Press.

The Power of Light: Eight Stories for Hanukkah by Isaac Singer, 1980, Farrar, Straus & Giroux, Inc.

GA1079

BULLETIN BOARD:

Background: dark-blue paper

Border: paper candle flames

Place menorahs and student-created writings about the bulletin board area.

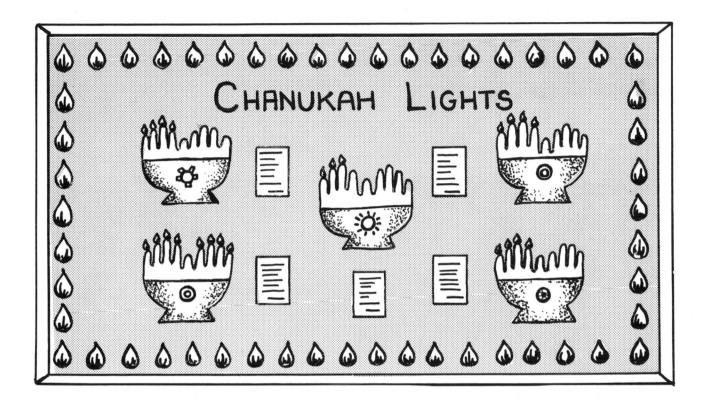

ACTIVITY: Taste as well as see the joy that is Chanukah. Consult your favorite cookbook and serve your students a special holiday treat. Latkes, or potato pancakes, might be enjoyed by all. Eat by the light of a menorah if possible.

WRITING ACTIVITY: The holiday of light celebrates the Jewish miracle that allowed a candle to burn for eight days on fuel that should have lasted just one day. By the light of a candle, have your students complete the following exercise to "brighten" the darkness of winter. Brainstorm things that a candle does as it burns. Children can choose from the many suggestions or add their own.

Burn little light . . . . (given)

shine on me

make me smile
⎫
light my way   ⎬   (student input)
warm my heart   ⎭

Teach me about Chanukah! . . . . (given)

GA1079

Mr. Ho! Ho! Ho!

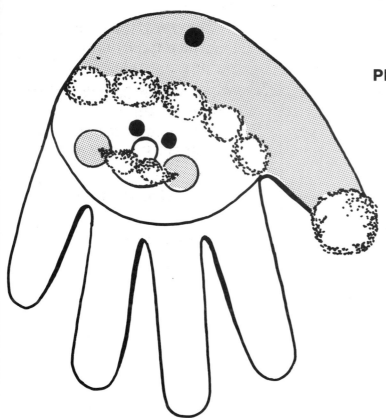

MATERIALS:
5" x 7" piece of pink paper, red and white paint, cotton ball, glue, hole punch, scissors, paper clip

PROCEDURE:
Paint the palm of each child's hand according to this diagram.

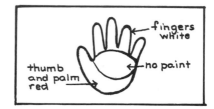

PROCEDURE: Press hand firmly on pink paper and let dry.

Be sure to turn hand so that fingers are toward the bottom of the paper.

In the center use crayon or thin black marker to draw Santa's face.

Add cotton ball trim for hat, mustache and small ball of cotton for pom-pom.

Punch hole in top of Santa's hat so he can be used as a tree ornament. Use paper clip to hang.

ACTIVITY: Play a Santa hand game this holiday season. You will need several small sacks. In each sack place a common item or small plastic toy. Let each child have a turn being Santa. Blindfold him and have him reach in a sack and identify the object.

When Santa fails to recognize an item, it is the next child's turn.

Have fun and remember to Ho! Ho! Ho! each time Santa fails to identify an item.

You could tie each sack tightly with green or red yarn. Each child tries to identify each item by shaking and feeling.

GA1079

BULLETIN BOARD:

Background: holiday gift wrap paper

Border: gift tags—one made out to each child

Place Santas about the bulletin board area.

Give each child a gift bag pattern. On the brown pattern the child should glue pictures of gifts he would like to give family and friends. Pictures of items can be found in old magazines and catalogs.

ACTIVITY:

Give each child the opportunity to play Santa or be Santa's helper. Make a list of ideas. The ideas should focus on things that could be done to make the holidays just a little nicer for someone. Let each child choose what he would like to do and share his idea with the class.

BOOKS TO ENJOY:

Santa's Christmas Journey by Roger Brooke, 1984, Raintree Publications.

The Night Before Christmas by Clement Moore as told by Tomie de Paola, 1980, Holiday.

Polar Express by Chris Van Allsburg, 1985, Houghton Mifflin.

GA1079

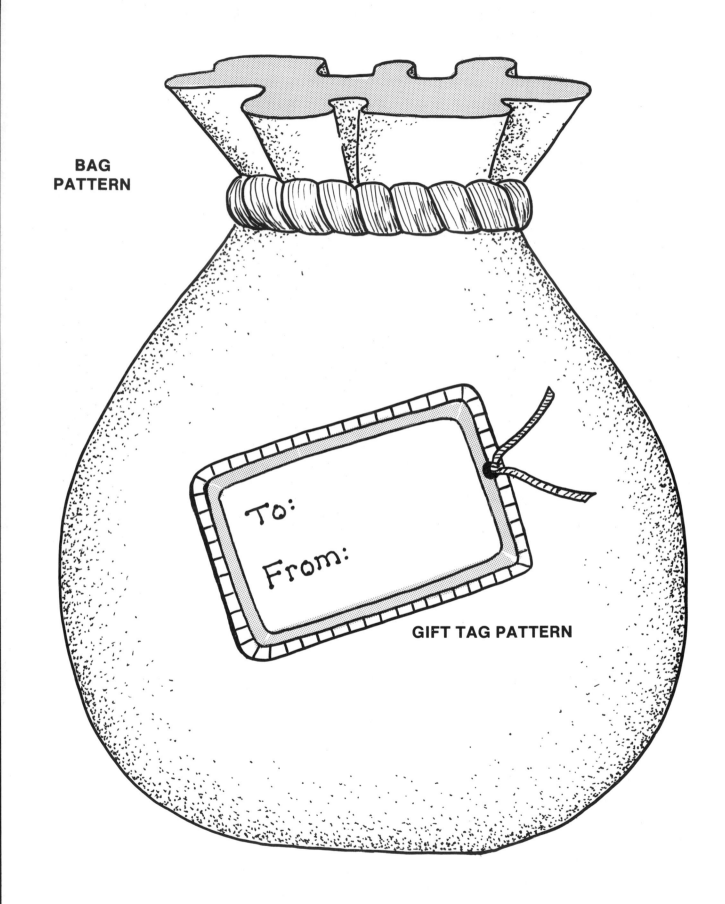

**BAG
PATTERN**

To:

From:

GIFT TAG PATTERN

96

GA1079

— A "Handy" Classroom Tree —

Here is a bonus project, and every child in your class or even every child in your school can contribute. Make a large wall, door or hallway Christmas tree. Trace each child's hand on a piece of green paper. Cut out the hands and glue them together as shown below.

Add snow to each branch by dipping a sponge in white paint.

Cut 3" circles from various colors of scrap paper and use to decorate your tree.

Cut a tree-topping star from yellow paper or gold foil and place at the top.

Remember to have each child print his name on his hand.

Holiday Salute

MATERIALS:

5" x 7" pieces of red and green construction paper, a 4" pink circle cut from construction paper, glue, scissors, crayons

PROCEDURE:

Place hand upright with fingers and thumb held tightly together. Trace the outline on either the red or the green paper.

While cutting out, square off the heel of each palm to shape the top of the soldier's hat.

Add a plume cut from the opposite color of construction paper. An alternative would be to use a bright feather. These can be purchased at most craft stores.

Glue completed hat onto circle and add facial features.

Glue entire soldier's head to a large sheet of paper and add body outline for students to color.

ACTIVITY:

Acquaint your students with the story of *The Nutcracker Suite*. Read the students the story or show a video of the ballet.

This should be done in several sittings, reading and viewing only highlights.

Focus on the section about the toy soldiers.

Form your students into a holiday brigade complete with paper hats. Decorated cardboard tubes could serve as magic wands used to protect the holiday gifts.

March about to the parade music.

98

HOLIDAY SALUTE

BULLETIN BOARD:

Background: any holiday gift wrap paper or a red and white striped paper

Border: small candy canes for the children to enjoy at a later date or big, bright green holly leaves

Attach the toy soldiers in military rows. Each student's creative writing efforts can be placed by his/her soldier.

*The toy soldiers would also look attractive lined along the chalk tray, as a border around the classroom or just outside the classroom door along a normally dull corridor wall.

WRITING ACTIVITY:

Children spend much of December anxiously waiting for that holiday that seems to come so slowly. Help them pass the time by writing about this eager anticipation. Be soldiers on guard, jotting down all signs of the season. Use the model below to create student-dictated writing.

I'll watch for signs of Christmas . . . .(given)

> bright lights that twinkle
> happy children that wait
> busy moms that cook

(student input)

They tell me that Christmas is near. . . . .(given)

BOOKS TO ENJOY:

The Steadfast Tin Soldier by Hans Christian Andersen, 1983, Little, Brown and Company.

The Angel and the Soldier Boy by Peter Collington, 1987, Knopf.

GA1079

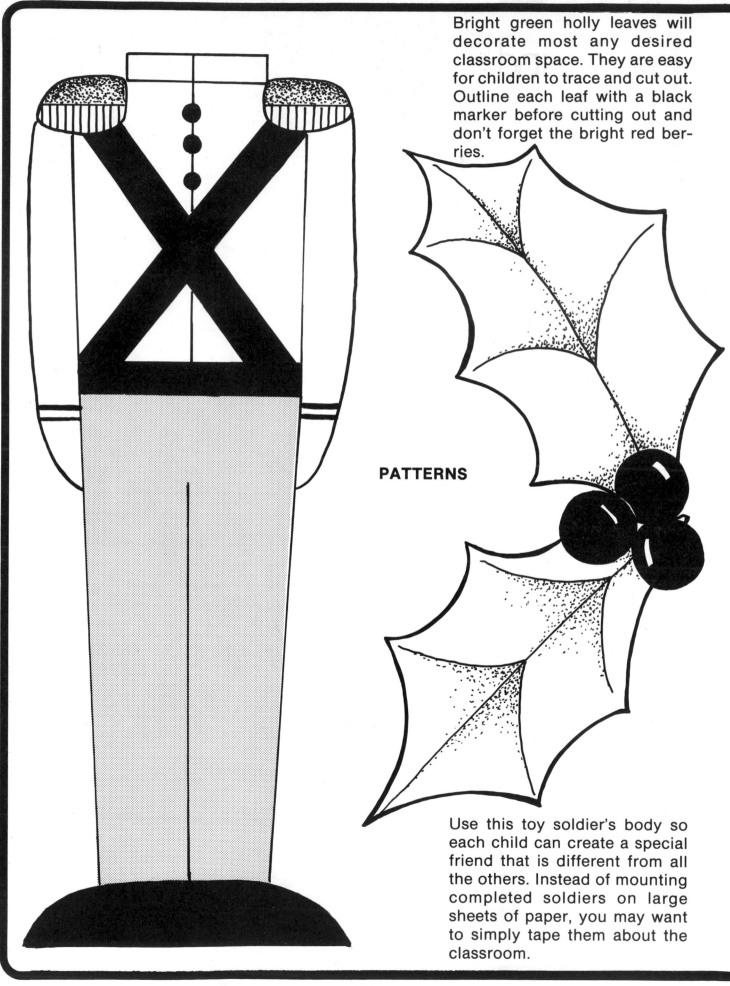

Bright green holly leaves will decorate most any desired classroom space. They are easy for children to trace and cut out. Outline each leaf with a black marker before cutting out and don't forget the bright red berries.

PATTERNS

Use this toy soldier's body so each child can create a special friend that is different from all the others. Instead of mounting completed soldiers on large sheets of paper, you may want to simply tape them about the classroom.

— A "Handsome Holiday Wreath —

All your children can be involved in creating this special holiday wreath that can be placed on the classroom door. Trace both hands of each child. Add white paint with a sponge. Outline hands with a black marker and cut out. Overlap hands slightly and tape or glue to create wreath shape. Add a bright red bow and a few red berries. What a personal way to say "Season's Greetings" to all people in your school.

GA1079

Heavenly Hands

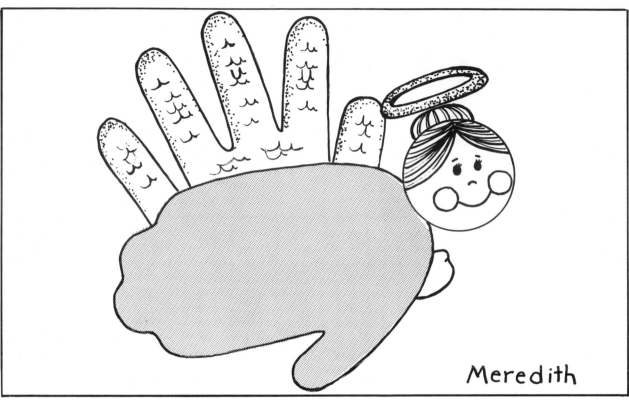

Meredith

MATERIALS: yellow, blue and pink paint; white drawing paper; crayons; glue; glitter

PROCEDURE: Paint each child's hand yellow and place it upright and slightly diagonally on the white drawing paper. Let dry.

Paint the other hand of each child pink or blue and place it thumb down (fingers closed) across the palm of the yellow handprint.

With crayons make an angel face. You may choose to use a photo of the child.

Lightly draw a halo. Cover outline with glue and sprinkle glitter on the glue.

BOOKS TO ENJOY: *Littlest Angel* by Charles Tazewell, 1946, Children's Press.

The Littlest Angel Earns His Halo by Ron Kidd, 1985, Ideals.

GA1079

BULLETIN BOARD:

Background: sky blue paper

Border: gold or silver tinsel garland

Create large fluffy clouds of cotton on the bulletin board area.

Attach student-made angels on and about the clouds. The angels should be holding student-made vocabulary/spelling lists.

Letters for this bulletin board could be made from gold foil paper.

ACTIVITY ONE:

Fold an 8½" x 11" piece of construction paper in half to create a large greeting card. On the front make the handprint angel described on the previous page.

On the inside print a holiday message. For example, "Handfuls of blessings come your way this holiday."

ACTIVITY TWO:

Let each child create a list of holiday words. Each list will be somewhat different because the words will be ones that the student can spell and use in a sentence.

Short lists are acceptable. Encourage each child to add a new word to his list each day.

GA1079

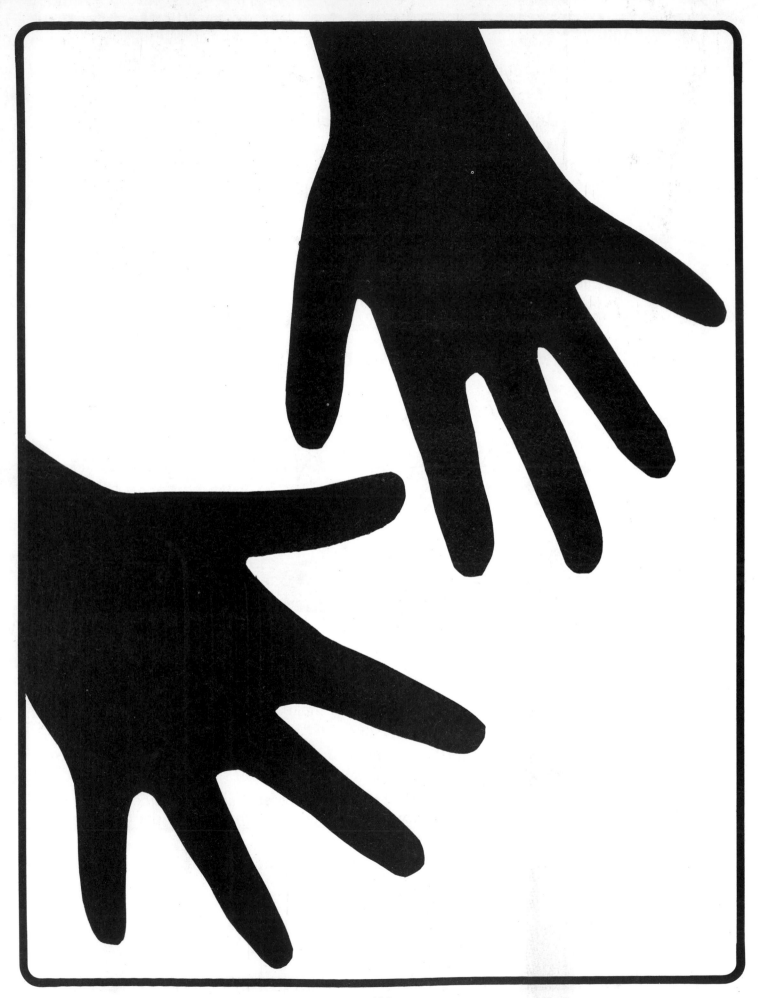